Thru Shai's Eyes
I

By:

Heru Smith

Parker's Poetry Plus Inc. First Edition 2022
Thru Shai's Eyes
Copyright © 2022 by Heru Smith
Published in the U.S.A. by:
Parker's Poetry Plus Inc. Brooklyn, NY
Written solely by: Heru Smith
Cover Concept: Heru Smith
Cover Artwork by: Kozakura (Fiverr)
Format: Parker's Poetry Plus Inc
Editor: Parker's Poetry Plus Inc
ISBN-13: 978-1-64713-789-2
Printed in the United States of America
www. ParkersPoetryPlus.com

Forward

We have all heard the statement, "everyone was born with a gift."

The dilemma is finding that gift and delivering it. After listening to Heru's Spoken Word, you realize what his gift is, and you see that he has a powerful delivery.

Heru's first book, leaves you with curiosity about your own gift, and it will certainly help you discover yours by reading his insightful poems.

Quote from Michael Gaddy

Acknowledgment Confession

This book would not be what it is without certain people playing their part in the production. Sometimes, the ones closet to you has the biggest impact on your life and push you to fulfill every dream imaginable. Connection means everything to me because you do not get to where you are without help from another. This is why I must acknowledge the help when it was beneficial for my growth. Therefore, these are the people who pushed me to be great: Renee Smith, Sarah Smith, Charles Rogers, Michael Gaddy, Nneka Smith, Imani Gaddy, Keisha Rogers, Quinell Kemp, Malcolm Gibbs, Ta'rasea Pankey, Aiko Roudette, Shanay Elliott, Justin Andrews, Maurce Colemen, Alvin Russell, Kozakura from Fiverr, Jan-Cheri Mears, Nicole O'Neal, Shakema Quarles, George Freeman, Brittany, Rixen Tarikh Emeka Campbell, Jawanza Phoenix, Daniel Norales, Jordan Hendricks, Kwame Gaddy, Curtis Harris Dorian Howard, Jive Poetic, Kiaji Simmons Beckles and Joel Parker. Thank You for Everything That You Have Done!!

CONTENTS

CONTENTS P<small>AGES</small>

CONTENTS   PAGES

(Cont'd)

Introduction

Thru Shai's Eyes

Imagination Pt. 2

My imagination will talk to you
And it will tell you what is on its mind
It goes like this:

Touching this face with working hands
just in case connection becomes extinct
While sitting on a sandcastle
looking for structure and not intimidation
Life is very beautiful if you happen to sit still
Thinking can be secondary
if you treat it like a manual for a new phone
While listening is one of the only instruments that is free 99
The past is an adult overseer
that has the same attributes of a psychologist
When I put up this image what do you see?
The future is an embryo that needs the proper incubation;
Sun, food and not your suffocation
So hold children close because
they're the virus to repetitive copycats
And watch how the present wants your cooperation
like doing yoga on yoga mats
What if the English language didn't like your culture?
To separate the vibrations and frequencies
from the community
Since in order for you to take the spirit out of something
you must remove the roots from its soil

Imagination Pt. 2 *(Cont'd)*

Can you sense the complete agony of discomfort
in these lines that needs a white background to get noticed?
Because your footprints aren't being the savior that your
traumas can find sincerity from
Since rum, oh wait I mean spirits, can be
an alternative way to speak to your ancestors
Not only to slow down the brain's receptors
 so one's unbiased truth can get attention
So, I guess there is the problem that I must confess
I'm too busy trying to help you contemplate life
from my own mortality

Never Going Broke

I guess you are wondering what does he mean by broke
I guess you are wondering
if it never actually has an expiration date
So maybe this is going to be difficult to digest
Like killing animals without the exploitation of
"Look at what I just caught!!!"
Could it be the pockets lacking the green hue for comfort?
Since they seem to go hand and hand
like peanut butter and jelly
While being famous is the mask that people put on
to disguise the unrealistic version of success
Could it be the infatuation of improving something
that is being copied from generation to generation?
Since a flower is
everything in itself of what beauty tries to duplicate
Since a baby knows nothing but
the experience of what it forgot
Could it be the itchy feeling of holding onto something
because somebody else says it has value?
Since some people will tend to
follow a lie that seems truthful
Since their tone of voice sounds promising to a
Culture-less mind
Would it be the excessive anxiety of having to
follow with closed eyes?
Can it be the end process in the definition of successful?
So people can put it on their resume as an accomplishment
In a system where your first choice is failure

Never Going Broke *(Cont'd)*

And the second choice having you giving up on you
to look important
Or will it be a means for the opposite of broke?
But how many people know what the opposite of broke
actually is?
Because the word in itself is put together from a man-made
production of letters that the majority are used to hearing
like an intentional tape recorder
for someone else's personal interests
That isn't interested in the well-being of everybody
Only to make sure that the existence never disappears
But my surroundings seem broke
The buildings are fixed to benefit the value of the
environment while pushing out the neighbors
who's only interest is living
The pavements look more broken up than crumbled up
cookies that were forgotten in my backpack
Transportation from A to B is becoming the same amount
as this cellphone bill
Help has a price tag on it
that no longer has the respect for connection
The school's pamphlets don't seem to involve unlocking
the true potential of its members
But people would rather be identical with the stars seen on
the television than the person living in their head
So is there anything that can be done?
There is a system that needs you to be
what it can keep tabs on

4

Never Going Broke *(Cont'd)*

It doesn't need individuality
It isn't interested in morality
It praises mortality
It does not appreciate organic experiences
It is allergic to choosing between two opposite possibilities
Even if everyone is born with both
So a virus will be needed to be created
One that should
counteract the disease that is being inhaled like oxygen
One that
jail breaks the program that was infiltrated from selfish
desires of wanting to destroy everything that isn't itself
I wonder if that is where self-hate was formulated ?
So maybe that is where self-intervention is looked at as
appalling
So there is seriously a big difference between
misguided and broke
But what if you aren't neither one of the two?
Or could it be that you forgot who you were
Because someone else programmed you
to become less than who you actually are
So, with all that said and done,
when will dismantling the system become a top priority?

The Death Culture Pt. 1

Man it is a shame what eyes are willing to see
It is heartbreaking to the soul to witness unnecessary pain
We attempt to paint different pictures
from the same outcome
Some even ignore the unjust memories
that the past endured
And still
the past found a way to provide shade for the present
And still the savage games are being played
from individuals just using different outfits
This cannot have a positive outlook on human beings
This cannot digest right on a stomach of morality
So who wonders what TV show is being replayed
more than it is being asked to?
People dying without a cause
A cause that has a reason
with no sense of belief backing it up
People are dying
because the fact that true power resides within
while despair transforms into the lever
for which the cage door opens
Some people even dying from excessive danger,
so their animal instinct becomes the bed they lay on
It is sick to see abuse get an acting deal
Like it is cool to let these lenses
oh I mean camera phones record and distribute fear

The Death Culture Pt. 1 *(Cont'd)*

Make protection actually be
forcefully protecting you from you
While the natural law of protection
gets swept under the cement
Since some say, "what you don't know won't hurt you"
Well we cannot see carbon dioxide, but it still can harm life
Guess not everyone wants to eat that GMO fruit

Connecting the Flames

You wonder
what the broken glass on the ground around us is for
The news feeds barbarianism to a culture
that only knows connection
But has lost itself due to brute force and **mental beatings**
The cameras only show what it doesn't what to hide
While displaying a movie because
most people are interested in entertainment
And, yes, in order for someone to be attained
someone else has to enter
But you're confused at the flames
trying to convince creation
The positive attributes of destruction
You want peace
but afraid to use hands and feet to demand it
You say the justice system doesn't protect the innocent
But refuses to contradict the fact that maybe, just maybe
your own thoughts aren't naturally your own
Information that is only seeking attention
is thrown around like a basketball,
but no one questions the person who is passing the ball
But you don't question what is being pumped into the ball
You just want justice to be for all
While failing to see that every teammate isn't on your team
Since the complexion doesn't necessarily bring loyalty
You're afraid that these buildings will fall and crumble

Connecting the Flames *(Cont'd)*

While most people who share your hue aren't even
qualified to own one for themselves
Because being a servant
is the only sufficient job that is up for hiring
And you're, deeply, hurt by individuals
who don't seem to think for their own
Well, perhaps,
maybe
they're finally annoyed that someone don't want them to
So riot reasoning must need a new unbiased definition
in order for closed eyes to actually trick the taste bids
into digesting the truth that has no seasoning
So it goes past the fact that
togetherness looks seemingly relatable
It lives above colors
so no one can add race into the equation
It is disgusted with him vs her
since most have the mind state of
"Make sure you get yours because I'll definitely get mine"
Since you uncontrollably act
without the brain questioning the purpose of its action
With success being measured by
how much you run after something that is man-made
While failure is a light switch
that is not coded with your fingerprint
So rioting introduces a new form of justice

Connecting the Flames *(Cont'd)*

Because its purpose is to eliminate its copycat
That wasn't programmed to have an interest in everyone
Only to make control feeling tolerable and acceptable
Therefore, rioting may not look desirable
You may question their rational actions
And you most likely will look at them in distaste
But, note that you don't want to fight on the forefront
Because your personal life has selfishly become a religion
Even if you want to see it or not

Caged Potential

We tend to worry about what he had in the past
We, sometimes question his habits
as if there isn't an end goal
He acts out of reality with his thoughts
Like if his purpose out ways the physical attributes
That Keeps him in touch with what he can touch
The trials and error get overlooked
by what he is taught to do
The why that gets overlooked
Is that his cries get drowned out with
"Suck It Up cause You're a Boy"
Which clouds the judgement
wondering the purpose of tears
He has lessons of what to be
He had lessons of what not to be
And he even had to partake in lessons of how to subdue
while forcefully attempting to digest what he is
Society masked abuse with
the musical tones of protecting a caged lion
So the potential looked inorganic
to a cage full of possibilities
In order for it to not recognize its true fixation
Of its true understanding of the hand it plays on destiny
Of the intellectual capacity it has that has to be experienced
Because words limits its strength to words

Caged Potential *(Cont'd)*

It is the Will that makes individuals
afraid of what's to come
It has to be the body odor
that sent her heart into a frenzy
Some say he need to be experienced
with uncontrollable thoughts
While others have to keep him sleep
so he cannot comprehend his existence
Since in order for light to know itself
Darkness has to be its starting point
This journey has taught him that you cannot
latch onto a substance that is outside of self
That radiates the need for its reflection
to know that it actually exists
How can she blossom
if the feeling doesn't
complement its intention?
How can femininity reach its peak of euphoria
if the mirror's duty doesn't involve masculinity?
While wondering if interaction will ever
take over justification
In order for authentication to get a chance at
building a character
Since he isn't interested in fitting in
Because human nature gets substituted for abilities

Caged Potential *(Cont'd)*

They whisper how **Shai** he has become
from the leaked insecurities
that paints distorted images of what he should do
But have forgotten his purpose due to what he admires
And not what illustrates the realization that she embodies
what he creates
So think of independence as a virus
with loneliness being its outcome
Therefore, be disgusted at how
independence is pretty selfish and hollow
And remember what it feels like falling back on comfort
As if hands never thought about letting you fall
Since connection
looks way more promising than you and I
So let the rough edges here solve that confusion
that sits on top of your crown
The thing is that he has to know himself internally
In order for her to acknowledge its significant other
That brings stability, guidance and closure
not an avenue for materialism to prosper

Togetherness Isn't an Illusion

You say there isn't any change happening
in front of both eyes
But blood was shed even if you cannot see it
You don't like your surroundings
but the people before made certain locations easier to live
You say that you are afraid to go outside
even after a specific time
While the past generations feared everything
every time they opened their door,
you illustrated that you want a better education
for your children,
when your great-great grandparents just wanted one
Since reading or writing was prohibited
She said she is having a hard time getting noticed as an
equal on the job
While when your grandpa was young,
he was trying to figure out if he was human or not
He cannot realize how come he does the same work as a
CEO but his paycheck highlights
the same attributes as a McDonald's cashier
But your mom's great grandmas' only occupation was
raising other people's babies
Since her own wasn't important to the
sports driven majority
They say applying for a job to help others in need is biased

Togetherness Isn't an Illusion *(Cont'd)*

When your 95-year-old grandfather
couldn't tell the difference
between a sheet to keep him warm at night
and a sheet that keeps burning crosses on his lawn
You say that most neighbors in your neighborhood
that look like you are getting kicked out
While your great forefathers knew
that if they crossed a line for justice alone
they would be shot or lynched in cold blood
And you wonder where a selfie came from
But not because of survival
but due to a high demand of distributing fear
So why must you think that the people before
didn't make the yellow brick road?
Could it be that you aren't interested in past digressions?
Or it is that individual selfishness
clouded your perception of togetherness?
Maybe it is realization
that you forgot how to pay homage to your ancestors
But they haven't lost the fact that
in order for change to happen
sacrifice has to be endured so that the next can actually live
with living being its pamphlet
Because you seem to think that the only Wall Street
had white people orchestrating the currency of funds

Togetherness Isn't an Illusion *(Cont'd)*

When Black Wall Street had its own community
to strive before it got burned down
She thinks that women aren't equal
to their male counterpart
When a female warrior by the name of Yaa Asantewaa
who had an army of over a thousand fearless fighters
who fought against the British
to make Ghana a safe haven to live with one another
He is finally getting the courage to stand up
against the killings of people that share his complexion
All he has to do is look up to strong men like Shaka Zulu
for strength but harbor his willfulness
While mixing it in with your will to fight for justice
with peace and correctness being the only mentor
that change cannot ignore
So the only person that is getting in the way
of your own people has become your own fear
that someone else's perception infiltrated your mind
Unconsciously that is
So, how about you actually think for yourself?
And kick out the tradition
that is only interested in self-division

Nameless Bullets aka The "Marriage"

Holding this weapon in both hands with confusion
of what relationship it has with me
It is heavy to the point where the muscles in my arms
shake out of uncertainly
Finger prints angry at the fact
that it can be in two places at once
Legs quivering from the sound of
"Put Your Hands Up Now!"
Eyes in extreme danger at the disbelief that this weapon is
the same complexion as mine
Nose getting that forceful second hand high from the smell
of the gun smoke
that was initiated from someone else's culture
Ears embarrassed
that the sound waves don't involve morality
Only "Today a young man was shot
and the only thing that he was holding
was a bag of skittles!"
Only "Today a black man was choked out
and you can hear him saying was
"I can't breathe"
Only "Today a woman dies in the custody of the police
but it seemed like she poses no threat"
Stomach tormented at this digestion period
that intimidated the pores to digest torment
Mind trying to process a bird's eye view
of the scenery around

Nameless Bullets aka The "Marriage" *(Cont'd)*

So an unjust action doesn't become recorded
from a society that is only interested in going left
While going right stays behind the scenes,
so it never gets caught with its hand in the cookie jar
Soo, what is this weapon
that my subconscious is so used to seeing?
It is used to protect the ones who are scared
It is used to install this cable television show called fear
Since it doesn't exactly exist, therefore pain and despair
becomes its attributes to make it feel and seem real
What is this safety lever for? Is it supposed to
stop the bullet from becoming a name and face
But a lot of people seem to shoot at the mirror
rather than out of defense
But it seems that it is aimed at someone who's only interest
is including justice in the justice system
Since friendly fire is an oxymoron for
shooting someone with the mirage of friendship
Man, what is this clip in this weapon for?
They say it holds 8 bullets for one, 5 for another,
and 12 for an extra clip if needed
So the question is, who is really being exterminated?
The one who has a lighter shade
or the one who has a darker shade
While realizing that they reflect the same light
when it hits the prism and refracts
What is this muzzle on it for?

Nameless Bullets aka The "Marriage" *(Cont'd)*

I even heard they got this plant called a potato that is used
to silence the sound as well
I wonder if they know that they're shooting nature and self
Since they both are one
Well, I did, actually over heard that it is called a gun
It is used to steal, kill, force unhealthy actions onto the
innocence and to confuse
The difference between a prey and a predator
So instead of shooting a man-made instrument at the next
generation
Aim your mind at elevating the ones who are having
difficulty with their reflection
Use the scope to zoom into their negativity with pure
positive thoughts
And extinguish the self-hate that is being pill popped like
antidepressants
Therefore, what if the greedy mind was put down for a
change and the intellectual one being picked up
Maybe the only shootings that will be seen are connecting
of the dots of unity
Maybe fathers and mothers won't have to burry so often
With the opposite actually looked at as thoughtful
With togetherness being the backbone of the cause
Because selfishness, greed and holding grudges no longer
needs to have a membership to our club

Graveyard Conversation

Let me take this seat here with unforgiving promises
While avoiding the harsh ingredients of the truth
Therefore, let me pop open this bottle
that doesn't have my best interest
Only my liver begging to be recognized for its filter stages
But let my emotions get a chance at dissecting reality even
if it is wearing Sunglasses
Since the whole doesn't know how to be wrong
While wondering if it is the ego
or if our parents were selective with their information
So as I sit, in this chair, I wonder who will save this hateful
resentment for accountability
Only myself and the uncut silence of honesty
Only myself and responsibility
who didn't come with a manuscript
Since the only person you can't fool is YOU
So I need your strength
to convince my actions that they supposed to be genuine
I need your guidance,
so selfishness doesn't carry the burden on my careful heart
But unity has become that one stone
that hasn't been turned over because
It lives outside the notion of getting the bag
While competition gets a paycheck every month
for its contribution to division
With the exaggerated attention that's becoming overrated
like following a trend, since everyone is doing it

Graveyard Conversation *(Cont'd)*

And intentions only seem to get contributed
when fraud is being highlighted
So stop dressing up what is acceptable like society makes
the English language do
Stop letting pride make its interpretation of what you think
happiness should entertain
So let's lean back without any respect for the spinal column
Only to make these words leak out constantly like pouring
liquor on the ground
Since everyone deserves some form of peace from another
Because strength comes from helping others
Not stepping on that same person so this paper called
degree is in reach
You showed me that the grass need water to function
You taught me how important earth stays together in order
to sustain life
You made me realize that peddles need air to improve its
transportation
And you made me appreciate that fire doesn't only cause
destruction
But creation as well
Well, I bet you are wondering why I'm speaking with
respectful feelings
Since logic is so one sided and it always needs to be right
I come to you in finding the importance of life
Some say it is for success

Graveyard Conversation *(Cont'd)*

And others say it is for the unforeseen generations to come
But what if it is to actually see that self is salvation
So togetherness can respectfully become the new formula
That individuals can practice monthly without a greedy
payment plan being its support system

The Gun

Ring! Ring!
Hey, what's up Rus said Damien.
I didn't see you in class today and we were supposed to
check out the new arcade that opened.
I know, but I overslept and by the time I woke up
it was lunch time, so I stayed home.
But guess what I found on my father's safe? Said Rus.
It is a safe for a reason right Rus? Said Damien.
Yeah, I know bro,
but you know that I'm nosy with finding things said Rus.
Remember the time when I got Christmas presents
and couldn't wait until Christmas,
so I opened the gifts the day before.
Yeah, I remembered that day and you tried to wrap the
gifts over so your parents wouldn't notice.
You are crazy for that bro said Damien.
But this is different,
so come over my house so I can show you said Rus.
I'm on my way now
and don't take forever to open the door
because I am down the hall; and, you're lazy
when it comes to opening doors said Damien.
Ha ha, you funny son,
well make sure you put some powder in those kicks
because your feet be humming said Rus.
(5 minutes later) Knock! Knock! Who is it said Rus.
It is me Damien open up the door already.

23

The Gun *(Cont'd)*

Hold on dude damn,
let me open the door for you first said Rus.
Where is your mom and dad at? Said Damien.
Do I ask you these types of questions
when I come to your Crib? Said Rus.
Um, yes every time;
you are quite nosy if I might say said Damien.
Anyway, come in my room
so I can show you what I found said Rus.
Damn bro your room is messy as hell, and it looks like
a tornado ran through your room, two times;
you got clothes everywhere,
your hamper smells like death, but hey your kicks are clean
though said Damien.
Ha, ha, you got jokes,
but at least my breath, don't smell
like eggs and athlete's foot said Rus.
Can we hurry this up bro, because if you keep stalling
then I don't want to see it anymore said Damien.
Close your eyes and I'll go get it said Rus.
Fine, my eyes are closed; now what it is
that you want to show me? Said Damien.
Open your eyes and peep this
that my father hides from me and my mom said Rus.
Is that a gun bro? Said Damien.
Yes, bro, it is a Glock 19.
Do you want to hold it? Said Rus.

The Gun *(Cont'd)*

No, I don't! I have seen a friend of mine
who got murdered by one two weeks ago
and I'm still a little traumatized by that said Damien.
My dad said that a gun is for protection purposes only
and not for installing fear into another person's mind.
And you know that where we live,
people get shot or killed every other day said Rus.
Well, my dad said that the gun isn't the problem,
it is the person's intentions behind the gun
that makes you question their purpose.
Anyways bro,
why are you showing me his gun for? Said Damien.
I want to protect you from your stepfather
and since the police is not helping then I will say Rus.
Ha, ha, ha, ha, stop playing with me bro,
you can't even kill a roach
and you want help me says Damien.
Yes, I do because we look out for each other
whenever there is a problem.
Remember the time when Tisha used to like me,
but didn't know how to say it, so she would beat me up
almost every day in 3rd grade? Said Rus.
Yeah your dad told you never to hit girls,
but I never got that message, since my father wasn't around
so I told Tisha if you hit my bro again
there will be problems says Damien.

The Gun *(Cont'd)*

Yeah, that was really crazy bro.
Or the other time I almost got in trouble
for putting glue in the teacher's chair,
but you distracted the teacher long enough
for me to get another chair said Rus.
Yeah, I remember that too;
but you stay trying to get into trouble
so you can be the center of attention said Damien.
So, are you going to let me shoot your step dad,
because he keeps abusing your mom?
And I know you see her face after they argue said Rus.
No! Said Damien.
Why not? Said Rus.
I already lost my real dad
because my mom pushed him away
since she didn't think he was strong enough to handle her.
So I don't want to lose anyone else that is close to me.
But I love my mom
and I don't know how she would react to that bro
said Damien.
Then how about we go watch Kung Ku Panda 3
and I'll go pop some popcorn in the microwave? Said Rus.
Fine, but let me go tell my mom where I'm at
so she won't get worried about me said Damien.
Aye Damien said Rus. Yeah! Said Damien.
Let's keep this between us says Rus. Fo'sho said Damien.

26

Let's Inject This

Come get comfortable in this seat that I built
Don't mind the straps here
Just in case you decide to involve intuition for a change
So come here and pull out your arm with relaxation
entering your comfort zone
Because my hands are warm
so let's see if it brings down your awareness
Breathe easy in the seat and stretch out your legs some
Now you may feel a little pinch
But don't mind the fact
that you do not wonder what is in the needle
I know that this humble presence seems supportive
And the stories that we converse over
was only part of the act
To lower the force field called common sense
Now don't worry about the negative videos
and conspiracies that make us look bad
So, no, fear isn't used
to decrease the strength of the immune system
And yes we actually care about your well-being
Even if the control of you makes it easier
to give you an outcome that makes you think
you have control over
And no we aren't interested
in making your frequencies low enough
to where hate fuels the feet to act
without the consciousness of the subconscious

Let's Inject This *(Cont'd)*

Therefore, leave the research to us
Since you no longer want to think for yourself
Your cellphones help you think
Your smart TV's listen as you think
So you wouldn't mine sitting in the passenger seat
As we make downloading our own algorithm
into your conscious seem friendly
But please don't resist the normal actualities of the images
that abused the rewind button
Yes, it is called the media
Yes, you see it on every new station
And yeah we say the same thing,
so just absorb what is being offered
But listen, it is only so you will never forget
and whenever a situation is formulated,
then you will stand back
with fear of hope of not getting the same treatment
And maybe, just maybe,
you will become a soldier for us to do good
for the ones who haven't been terraformed yet
But know that the killings were justifiable
So there isn't a need for any riot now
And how about leaving the awakening process to the plants
With already knowing that reading is considered obsolete
Therefore, question nothing
Accept what is given without any thought of contradiction
Because everything that is being done is for your own good

Follow The Fire

The print for self has been forgotten
The way to be, has been overturned by how to act
The way of living has been substituted for surviving
under someone else's circumstances
While the way your ancestors lived
are on display in museums
for everyone including self to get reassurance
But to you just a foggy mirror without clarification
Everyone sees the greatness but you
Everyone feels the true strength, but you are too afraid of it
Even if it is YOU that you are scared of
Everyone searches for spirituality
while you are born with it
And everyone's only interest is to live
with the underlining truth that is,
your beginning is to reach an end
And your end is only just the beginning
So there is a path placed in front of your mind
in order for your feet to follow
It doesn't need money to present fruit
Its intentions are pure
like a bird finding food to nurture its young
And it preserves help as a means of salvation
So if you are interested in appreciating life
Follow The Fire
The messages are on walls for you to see
The energy is there

Follow The Fire *(Cont'd)*

Just connect with another
For connection purposes only will be the key
Read from the text
Place yourself in it and live like you are reading you
Since a book is designed to place the individual within
While the author gets to predict the outcome
even if the story is about him
So overstand what that means and leave words to talking
Since feeling holds a stronger magnitude in understanding
the same experience from different perspectives
So see that you create cultures
And not stumble onto a lost one
You were everything
until you were forced to become a puzzle piece
You didn't need anything until your other half was forced
into thinking it was more important
And nothing had more value on it than reaching bliss
Until that green hue was introduced as false contact lenses
But you weren't born blind
So let me know when you are ready to follow the fire
Oh I seem to forget to mention
That the fire is already inside of you
Just listen for a change

Unorthodox Drug Dealer

Psss!
Hey, come here
Come here so I can show you what I have
No, I don't have anything to alter your perception
No, I don't have something to forget your reality
Even if reality is all in your mind
And no I don't have an escape from the pain
that you cannot get rid of
So I bet you're wondering
what is under this black trench coat
What if I said it isn't magic?
Would you digest it?
Or would you call me a fraud
because I'm stealing your intentions without a purpose
Well, I'll curb your enthusiasm
Can't believe you actually need a hint to yourself
It is a shame that one gets a blurry vision
when exercising the mirror to its full potential
It's understandable that society needs people to not think
It's okay if you need help
to express your natural power that is stored within
Not the mind
since mind control starts above the cerebral cortex
But... others call it the pineal gland
Hey now, I'm still a drug dealer
Just to let you know
But the purpose is not self-centered by human thoughts

Unorthodox Drug Dealer *(Cont'd)*

I guess you are wondering what I have for you?
It is a pill
Not the red pill, or the blue pill
Not a pill with more side effects than cures
But a pill that all religions swore to give
to help you endure the pain that made you who you are
It is called SELF
The one that a lot of people think video chat can fulfill
The one that makes cyber bullying think it is trending
Because being original is looked at as being irregular
I give you self with the unorthodox of not being identical
Since it is hard to control someone
who feels control as immoral
Just overstand that
once the human emotions are left behind
Now their true self actually gets a turn
You might experience the loss of fear
or the absence of apathy towards someone
who is only looking for Superiority
It makes one forget about the division of two
This is for the ones who know their true identity
And aren't hiding behind their own face
It will make you reform
to the heritage that the soul already knew before words
And help shed the skin that was forced with encyclopedias
But it will give you the thrill to protect the helpless

32

Unorthodox Drug Dealer *(Cont'd)*

Since people were more valuable than green bucks
at one point
So once you start thinking with self
then the values also change
Just ask the mirror for once
I bet people are wondering how much is this pill??
Well, if you wish to know
It is FREE
It doesn't cost anything to take the pill
Only the infatuation of losing it all
But what are you really losing
when everything is inside of you?
I'll tell you if you still are somewhat confused
Nothing!

Attractive Drug Dealer

You know what is needed
A WAY OUT!!
No way of getting one
Therefore, money controls these shaky hands
Greed is the passion that used this addiction
Smell of it cannot hide
Due to the long hours of brainwashing
No walls can trap this hunger
Only the illusion of falling into this quick sand called rehab
With calm being injected into the veins
to counteract the jitters
Words of change
from compassionate others having no affect
Affect the thought of loneliness not penetrating the mind
Grind every moment for that high
Objects around having a price tag
that feed this sweaty uncontrollable ambition
Kaleidoscope vision is what comes next
Feet becomes floating clouds
with the sky being the only future
Deaf ears becomes more sensitive to sound
Taste of information is now tasty to the tongue
Veins need that hit of destruction
It's the food that fuel these legs to move
I run, I dunk, I cycle, fastballs are thrown,
math is easy as pie, I hustle
Nothing can stop this hunger of being the best

Attractive Drug Dealer *(Cont'd)*

Do not test this perfectness
with shameful facial expressions
Love the fact that the future is being created
Admire that he or she does not care what people think
Blink and record his or her footprints
to realize that those shoes are too big for your mind
Find the blue prints if you dare
But note to self
Life is moving forward
just not the way you thought it would
While motion itself is amused with what happens next
With only the divorce of the hit tends to bring chaos
No remorse for anyone or anything if it enters the path
Wrath of greatness blinds the eyes to see nothing else
The floor plan is laid out as well as tattooed in the vision
The Only Real Enemy is the Drug Dealer
Would this happen if there was guidance from the start?
There Cannot be guidance if there is not a message behind
So if a problem surfaces in front
Stop the madness from the beginning
Words can be stepping-stones to levitate
As well as stab wounds that the naked eye cannot see
Or choose to do nothing from the well placed world
that was written out from birth
From what most people give off
without knowing, a single thought
Bring to life someone who is at his or her darkest hour
Now you are a real comic book hero

The Closet

Twin Flame

Ring-Ring!
Ring-Ring!
Ring-Ring!
Ring-Ring!
Ring-Ring!
Ring-Ring!
(Arguing with the thoughts in my head)
What if I crack my heart open,
can you will it with your light
So this left side of my brain can
stop getting in competition with its right
So I hope she answers the call
So she can see her reflection in me
through this confession of urgency
I'm not interested in the future
since it is outside the field of touch
But sensing the past neglect
that is trying to live on your back
like an annoying co-worker
With offering myself as a way out from the norm
So presenting this masculine as a gift
helps her feel comfortable being the opposite
While putting the insecurities on the big screen
so she can laugh at how identical we can become
I need her to breathe so I know where life began
She needs to jack-in without the 5 senses controlling
to see where Will comes from

Twin Flame *(Cont'd)*

So programming the heart to beat properly isn't that hard
My logic has a problem with feelings
because it seems to put itself in harm's way
My feelings have a problem with logic
because it is afraid to touch the spirit
So what is your situation?
I might be your past
scared at the fact that the footprints seem identical
Or could it be the noise in the background
fighting for attention with your physical
being its only importance
Or it could be
that some people who haven't experienced happiness
continue to drag you down
like a negative quick sand with nothing
But lies and deception controlling your life
like Virtual Reality
So why not give me an unbiased opportunity
to see if our souls can co-exist for a change
We might end up balancing each other out
while the universe appreciates the front row seat

Twin Fire

I want to start off by saying
I can't breathe oxygen properly
without you gazing into my soul
I have a problem with daydreaming
because I can't touch you properly
I have a personal problem with my personal world
You're not in it
It's your eyes that tells me
that the future is too long to wait for your love
It's your smile that makes my heart want to
talk without words for a change
With the blood using anticipation
to blind the brain
from thinking of what can happen next
So trust can finally stop being scared
at someone else caring for these intentions
It is your scent
that make these pores perspire out a mirage
of an identical twin
So loneliness becomes only but a word without a definition
Man, its' got to be your personality
that makes my ego bow down with respect
In order for self to recognize
what a mirror attempts to display
a physical version of

Twin Fire *(Cont'd)*

Called reflection
So itself can finally decide
that half isn't as satisfying as the whole thing
While wondering
if you will be able to accept that
when we intertwine, life gets to write itself
Because the artwork will always reflect the painter
Well, it has to be your laugh
that show these ear drums of mine
that listening is so secondary
Since you have to feel first before you can taste
But, what if it is your natural fragrance
that makes these nose hairs force the mind
into indulging in to darkness of where everything is created
So trust gets to finally open its pages of these feelings
So connection is interested in face to face interaction
While opening up myself to you
as if surgery isn't the only instrument displaying the insides
and giving access to the algorithms of my past;
so this logical computer Knows something
other than ones and zeros
They say he did it all for the sake of her
so her insecurities have a safety net for doubting itself
In order for "it's okay I'm here for you"
to have any significance

Twin Fire *(Cont'd)*

Because her flaws
missed the feeling of being asked out on a date
He said he did it for the sake of his own existence
So he has something to fight for
other than his selfishness
So his spirit
can hug her forceful misconception of competition
With the hope that this hue-man being
finally gets a glimpse at perfection
He's willing to expose all
so you can see what is hiding behind the mask
He's willing to put his love in a tape recorder
so the only real competition he has for your love is himself
And I did it for the sake of your love
Therefore, words sometimes speak
just as loud as actions do
And I don't just love you
I Love All of YOU!!!!

You Are My Life

I see your eyes and I always stare
Because there is a beautiful glare
I know you sense my heart
Because without you I will part
I love your smile I like your lips
It makes me never miss that scented kiss
I can wonder why but I won't need to cry
Because with you in my life
I now don't need to wonder about why
You make me stop crying because there is nothing to fear
Except dying but I don't want to die without your love
Because it's what I'm thinking of
Every day that I am not with you I'm here and I'll help you
think it through

Make It Be Seen

Wow!
Can't believe that the wish came true
Been speaking words into existence
with hopes of self-paying attention
to the desire of what it needs
For joy to actually balance out its partner, despair
So let the waves of energy
reflect this turbulence of excitement
While the soil beneath our feet
get nutrition from our interaction
of intertwining our DNA
so seeds can know what an origin looks like
Let the breath of life
see where it gets its determination from
So the physical and material planes
can see what authenticity looks like
And touch this heartbeat with the taste of your aroma
That saw the bread crumbs in the sand
back to your spirit with the sound of
You spilling my name all over your present
so these nose hairs can dissect
the difference between honesty and temptation
In order for the heart
to show the true characteristic of this **Shai** person
In order for this voice
to speak without the ego trying to glorify itself

Make It Be Seen *(Cont'd)*

With the mirror no longer needed
to show the beauty of what is in front of
what vision has a hard time grasping
Since it lives outside of sight
of what money has a hard time conjuring
the fact that some things
don't have a price tag that need reassurance
While lying in this bed of uncertainty
so logic is looked at as English brail
In order for the waters of femininity to
Kiss these lips
so these eyes can accept being blinded for a change
Hug this body close so
the pores can have a conversation with the skin
And no I don't mean perspiration
While nurturing these wandering thoughts
with realistic attention
Hey!
You!!
Can you hear the piano tones from my voice
trying to capture your intelligence?
Can you comprehend the level of growth
that was needed to be experienced?
So let's hope that this heart pulse
doesn't get caught in vein

Make It Be Seen *(Cont'd)*

Hopefully, this hunger for your mental don't seem thirsty
Only wanting to digest something real
Therefore, make it seem real
Hold this hand just in case these feet stumble
Pick him off the ground if his identification is still blurry
Let nature be his teacher besides your correction
It shows that you actually care
And that society might not have our best interest at hand
So let's create our own
Because you need me as much as I need you

Glad That You Called

Hey!
Hey!
Give me a minute to express the vibrations of my feelings
Let me explain why this heart has opened up
to all possibilities from your smile alone
Give me a chance to stop time through my honesty
And my uncontrollable thoughts of our worlds
living hormonally intersect
While we appreciate the fact that creation can only give
what it can interact with
I need you to appreciate that these words
need room to grow
Because when you start with crawling
you get a better feeling of what is holding you up
Since it gets better as you nurture them more often
Therefore, the movement of this internal existence
is eager to show you yourself
With the understanding
that maybe you are the glue to this fractured face
that is afraid of seeing its reflection
or was forced to accept someone else's
Or could it be
that these feelings actually aren't on the chopping block
So the past digressions can no longer become important
Since every second of the present
is an opportunity to see into its future

Glad That You Called *(Cont'd)*

Wait, no, I mean your eyes
because the future isn't as amazing as what is in front.
In front, of this heartbeat
who has become comfortable with beating Irregular!!
So you see that there is a confession
that wants to be relevant
I must confess that speaking with digestible truth
holds no regrets being its religion
Every rock starts off ruff
until water holds it with creation being its 911
With that being said
I open the key of my heart to your incubation
that craved to be your masculine side
to look back to you in satisfaction
So let us water the seeds that show opposition
Because that will always become food for thought
So that they need each other to exist
There is an infatuation with wanting to digest your pain
so happiness can have a go at the spotlight for a change
In order for stress to recognize that stress isn't that big
Because imagination is the only aspect
the future doesn't have a hand in
Since water doesn't need to crash to sculpture rocks
So justifying her flaws as scars on his skin
is deemed as
Thoughtful

Glad That You Called *(Cont'd)*

So she can see that boundaries are nothing
but movable chairs with the function of playing a game
And forgiveness is only a call on speed dial
So her sense of worry can infuse
with his diminishing image of himself
While our unbalanced sides
crave room to become balanced
Man his ears couldn't take the silence
But she finally called back
since she no longer listens to the wandering planets around
Therefore, these unrehearsed behaviors
can finally get a concert rehearsal,
without any interruptions
With hoping that she can see and feel
that all these actions
Aren't even rehearsed to begin with

Why Do You Love Me?

What do I do that makes you attracted to me?
I don't show any emotions
But yet you keep showing yours
I get mad when you don't be yourself
But you still call me
I have nothing to offer you in any way
But yet you say I have everything that you are looking for
The only thing that I am doing is being myself
But yet you tell me that's all you need
I don't tell you I love you
But yet you still say it to me
We are opposites in every way
But you're still attracted to me
I don't really talk that much around you
But you still wanna be on the phone with me
I'm not that funny
But yet you still laugh at my jokes
You still love me, but I don't love you anymore
It's time for you to move on
I'm not the man for you now
Our future together looks really blurry now
So I can't be your friend anymore
And this I know for sure
The only thing I can say to you now is
BYE-BYE

Who is Your Replacement?

Years were put in
They were put in to make perfection hate itself
Memories in the brain starting to become catalogs
Catalogs, with that destination not looking so bright
Catalogs, with the pictures fading from false promises
Feelings of emotions
hesitating on what feelings should feel
Since time was punched in everyday
and never thought about punching out
Since the house was built from the ground up
So the foundation would never crumble
So seeds could be planted
and have a fighting chance at survival
Sometimes happiness itself is taught to the ones
who can see that value of togetherness preceding surviving
Surviving, is
what everyone has possibly been programmed to do
But how many people are truly living?
Or going through their daily life
as a so called normal person
When every second was meant for that person to be happy
While every minute was valued as a wonderful experience
That regret will never understand
the purpose of its true power
So every hour was spent
on what our imagination had a hard time

Who is Your Replacement? *(Cont'd)*

Imagining what happiness felt like
With every day
we wished night time would let the day seemed longer
So every week discovering ourselves felt at home
like a baby being nurtured in the womb
While every month's time having difficulty
with predicting how much time was not being needed
Because every year her right
gets more comfortable with his left
So getting over that person looks pretty unimaginable
Unimaginable, not to a brain
that has creation flowing throughout its DNA
So is change possible to this regretful heart?
So what replacement is needed?
Maybe time should be like taking a cassette tape out
because it is full
And putting a new one in
Maybe letting the past memories become your
boy/girlfriend
Since giving up on the past gets confused with
giving up on life itself
Or maybe…just maybe it got crumbled up
because it was needed like a breath of fresh air
So will life keep moving
or will it become a photo in a picture frame on the wall?
If only the mind is willing to repeat these messy episodes
with a new main character

Can You See?

You're blind by the word "LOVE"
You can't see but you hate
You don't think of the phrase
"Do to other what you want them to do to you"
You can see but you're still blind
You only think of yourself
But gets angry when you see your girl/guy
with someone else
You can hear but you don't think about the consequences
You don't say am I doing wrong to him/her
but you think, ahh who cares
You say in your head that you going to act differently
but your body movements say yeah right
Your soul sends out negative vibes
You're a leach on other people's pain
that is never contained happiness
You keep on doing the things you do
Sooner or later you will be by yourself
confused by the path that you made

Abusive Materialism

Hey!
Hey!
In front of you
Yeah, I don't look like I can't afford you
I know you want me to take you out all the time
Even if my wallet is screaming for redemption
Tired of sticky hands appreciating these pockets because
Because their dream might be inside
Yeah, I don't look similar to your past impressions
Since they touched your skin out of fear
And I'll only touch your face
in an attempt to find Myself
Wait… wait don't leave yet, I'm not done
I want to know the purpose of that makeup
that needs to sit on top of your beauty?
Hopefully, you aren't afraid of your own reflection
Hopefully, your circle isn't catering to
what society thinks is pretty
Because your free will is all that is needed
to see through sensational illusions
Because once the door to the soul is open
you cannot help but to stitch mine up
Like nurturing a baby in the springs of nature
But what is the deal with
amputating on the definition of perfection

Abusive Materialism *(Cont'd)*

Just cause
someone on the television screen
who knows not the meaning of words
Who cannot tell the different
between themselves and a cable remote
Illustrate the identity of loving yourself
inside and out
You don't need to be fake to look attractive
You don't need to add on material to feel sexy
You don't have to sound loud to stand out in a crowd
You don't need to wear names to be important
You don't have to be picky in order to have standards
You don't need to win an argument to act intelligent
I stumbled into you
because the real you is inside somewhere
The one
before social media became the teacher of experience
The one
before opinions were tattooed on someone's character
The one who loves for the sole purpose of love
without looking for something in return
They say
"You give so your spirit smiles not your pocket"
So, I can be the one
who can restructure your hypothesis about a relationship

Abusive Materialism *(Cont'd)*

I could be
in front of you
On the side of you
Two steps behind
Or I could be
in arms reach
If after my confession
you don't question this materialism
that haunts your eye sight
Then that self-hate syndrome
is already plaguing your system
Alert!
Alert!
Intruder Alert!
Can you hear my concernment screaming out?
Guess not

Feminine Essence

See I don't know about you
But there is something about a strong woman
who you can put your pain on
and sunshine seems to sprout out somehow
Who can digest destruction and birth out creation
with a single tear of "I got this" on speaker
so this heart can beat regular
With hands of forgiveness
for this train wreck of broken promises
With feet that can travel to the end of time
to show devoted love
While caring for unforeseen generations
that are anxious to be developed
So this word called perfection can learn
that its definition is actually false
And a heart that loses its puzzle pieces
every now and then
But where knowing thy self is considered second nature
Which is when the real milk is looked at
as being the first study guide for connection
With what is pondering how can this be physically possible
When admiring from a distance the strength of power
that doesn't need to be masculine
Why must that voice act so loud?
Since the essence of fragrance
holds a greater magnitude for understanding

Feminine Essence *(Cont'd)*

So where did you go to?
How come you don't want to be yourself?
What is missed
is that push that makes a rock into a sculpture
What is missed
is that "I understand" that comforts ideas with sincerity
And what is truly missed
are the arguments
that are supposed to bring us together as a whole
Not divide us
through the confusion of the meaning of division
So within your darkest hour
we must express our generosity
with already knowing that words hold no water
But you deserve everything
that money tries to put a value on
Yes, you are being bombarded with how to be
And how to act,
which can slow down your uniqueness
But within all that smoke
you can still rise above it all
The key is to just be yourself
Learn to choose
between what is right and what is socially acceptable
Have the courage to stand up for what feels wrong

Feminine Essence *(Cont'd)*

Appreciate that you are needed
Even if the mirror is the one who is saying it
Know your worth
Take responsibility for your actions
Speak without letting the ego take control
It shows
a character that should be duplicated
It shows
that the actual you is better than the mask
that people portray
And it truly displays the beauty of the fact
that we need each other
In order for all to be treated equally
Don't let anyone treat you less than who you are
Carry yourself as if respect was a fragrance
So smile with strength, as much as the sun does
And know that there is a crown on your head
Even if no one else sees it
So stand up not because I said it is right
But because you want improvement as much as I do

Click to Send Flowers

How do you do this again?
I'm supposed to press a button so she can see me
Not who or what I really look like
But what the digital life want me to become
Is this really her picture here?
I can't tell if those are her real eyes
or if society conned her into changing it
What are these hearts for under this picture?
Someone told me that to show love you double click
But I can't feel anything
even after double tapping the screen
How can I really enjoy this artificial touch
since it is tricking these fingers into imaginary love?
And why are there so many websites to choose from
in order to send flowers?
Maybe this dollar here
is more important than the happiness of the receiver
Man, they need all my info just to show that I care
Maybe face to face dialect has become the new flip phone
Why is this monitor or cellphone block
the translator for my feelings for you?
Since you won't speak when I'm in your private space
Since your feed holds more attention than my intentions
And the only time our eyes lock in is on holidays
And most of the holidays aren't even ours

Click to Send Flowers *(Cont'd)*

It's crazy how
There are more pictures over the internet of you
Than trying to convince you
that no filter can express your beauty
Capturing perfection with a camera
is much better for generations after to reminisce over
While I'm looking for it in real time
There were moments in time
where both hands got jealous
of every time someone else touched your face first
Where the only moisturizer that was needed for these lips
was your tears
To where my real first tattoo
was your finger prints on my back
Which gave this heart easy excess
to the chambers of your existence
There was a time
when I remember ringing your doorbell almost everyday
And then jumped in the bushes
to wait for you to come out to see who it is
And then jump out screaming "SURPRISE!"
Just to get your heart to beat frantic
Wait, I mean so your heartbeat can get in sync with mine
Since your perfume never leaves this memory file cabinet
I remember giving you a gift and once you opened it

Click to Send Flowers *(Cont'd)*

You looked back into my eyes and said
Where is it?
And I say back "you're looking at it"
Soo!!
Can we finally start repeating the sequence of me
being your up and you being my down
While venting, pain being the personal needle
that makes patching us together
Much easier
More enjoyable
And less people in our world
Can we just go back?
Back to where the windows of our souls
are right next to each other
Because when I look into your eyes
impossible looks beautiful to an optimistic mind

Blue Hair

Blue hair like the river flowing
Flowing from the beautiful colors that it captured
Fracture only the boundaries of the words
"I CAN'T"
Blue hair like the clouds above us
Shapelessly floating in the wind with life
and commitment inside
Pride not needed because fault can own up to blame
Blue hair like the chair we sit in
Comfortable place where listening comes natural
Time sitting alongside
because it is more interested than passing by
Sober feet angry from the hours of sitting that was put in
Grin from the satisfaction
that the ears absorb so much information
Blue hair like blue fire
that someone tries to subside
The control factor that has no use
but used from being stubborn
Attractive to the thought of not being controlled
makes life interesting
Blue hair like the dress
when it hits every curve
Eyes stayed glued
from the confidence
of how sexy the body makes the dress look

Blue Hair *(Cont'd)*

Accessories and make-up
mad that the personality, helps them to stand out
Shoes acquire two left feet
from the unrehearsed dance moves
Blue hair like the covers
to keep us warm
Warm to where
the stars in the sky are not the only things sparkling
Comforting
to where the bed gets jealous
Romantic scenery
 to where the television looks at us,
as if it is at a movie theatre
Blue hair
is what everybody should experience
once in someone's life

Dip the Pen *(Cont'd)*

Man!!
It is hard to express these powerful feelings
When I'm close by,
the hairs on my back stick up like electricity
When I'm too far,
this masculinity sends vibrations of tasting your soul
Kissing you will feel like forever
No need for a memory bank
when you capture the reason to live
Oh my gosh!!
Those blemishes and insecurities are so sexual
I want them all
Maybe by writing this letter
She will be able to read this sexual invitation
How about writing with a pen, full of this ink
With a paper not as soft as your skin though
I need a starting
like, I want to record your heartbeat
So I'm actually moving to the sound of compassion
No not that…
Maybe, I want to get you pissy drunk
so the both of us can black out
Don't worry,
I'll be the light at the end of the tunnel
No, no, not that…

Dip the Pen *(Cont'd)*

Maybe, Let me touch you all over
so your clothes will get jealous
The covers will envy that these kisses are
More important than
the purpose of what the covers are used for
No, no, no, not that...
Maybe, Hey there beautiful volcano
I'm here to help you blow off some steam
No, no, no, no, not that one either ah...
Maybe, Hello Ms. Galaxy
Your mind is like the universe
It is going to be a voyage in exploring
and feeling everything
If you scratch me up, I don't mind
They're love marks to show other women
That "I'm All Yours!"
I don't care which other man tried to talk to you
This strong cologne scent
will send them running for the hills
The bed will become upset
because it is getting replaced tomorrow
Like all the exes before me
It's okay if you let the neighbors hear
I'm aiming to hit every spot
so seeing with your eyes closed can become Imaginable

Dip the Pen *(Cont'd)*

Don't pay attention to me being cocky
I tend to want to stand strong
Rubbing my hands up and down your skin
which causes friction
is the closest feeling to the enjoyment of getting a tattoo
Once you get one,
there is a strong possibility you will get another
Touching your curves reminds me of
the waves in the oceans
I don't only want to ride, but I want to own it
Here is my surfboard…
Cowabunga Dude!!
Then cover my body in the sand of your sexuality
Moisturizing my body in your love
So this half of soul is finally within reach
of that mysterious other half
Then after, bathe me in your water so I can grow
So I taste every emotion that exists in the universe
Hold on…Wait!!
Let me get my bib
Don't want to waste a drop
This life depends on it
so I cannot stop
So send back the address with a spray of your perfume
Because I think you will have to call in a leave of absence
Because one day is not going to be enough for this appetite

Not in Sight

See that there is no one like you
Maneuvering these feelings
to where they are working against the brain
Making the heart beat seem as loud
as a man banging his drum at Jay Street
waiting for the A-train
Showing affectionate temptation
through hoops of fire called jealousy
Leaving clues from smiles and hugs
lying round beneath our feet
So this blender full of mixed emotions
can actually become something promising
So this broken heart
will become useful finally
So this experienced mind
actually has something to learn for once
With only these shaky toes trying to fit in the shoes
that the elder had a hard time doing
No one in sight
Can blow wisdom into the eardrum
with no words from the English language
Makes jumping to conclusions
looked at as being compassionate
Makes the value of good being the finish line
from the mysterious games in real time
Makes texting "good morning" or "goodnight"
coming before Brushing the teeth in the morning
Or getting a full nights of rest

Not in Sight *(Cont'd)*

Yes, that simple peck on the cheek
will somehow make the hairs on the skin raise up
like being continuously electrocuted
There are strong qualities
and forgotten possibilities in chasing
It may show strength of wanting something real
Or it may help fill in a blank slide
from the forgotten experiences that needed paint
Or maybe and I mean hopefully
it can constitute fighting as being righteous
With only three outcomes being presented
on this chalkboard
    1) Being the one that has not been seen before or yet
    2) Looked at as identical to the pain that needs to be
       left in the rear view mirror
    3) Letting the memories dictate who is worthy and
       who is not
With a positive yet drunken outcome looking scarce
Well they say if the truth is needed then ask a child
or a drunk person
But no foreign substance is needed in being genuine
or truthful
Not a soul
Can over stand the sound waves that these two can hear
No need for words or emotions
Their aura is enough
From closure and connecting the spirits
With time aggravated that it is not part of progress

Not in Sight *(Cont'd)*

It becomes a timeless goal wrapped around "what if"
What if hardship only made the bond stronger?
What if everyone else never got the grasp of our affection?
What if the divine light is two different hearts
beating as one
So synchronize thought seems natural
Knowing that two souls actually see through one eye
Shows that one plus one
can only be two is when a child is manifested
So what else cannot be in sight?
Getting the courage to become a shoulder
for a tidal wave of tears
Making a human's ego
becoming a non-factor to a spirit's compassion
Letting the tongue which orchestrates words slow down
so the ears can feel the vibrations better
Kicking down this brick wall to let the heart
over-stand the importance of being vulnerable
Learning to control sight with touch,
cause even in darkness we can still feel
Spilling out the past unimaginable like a crack in a ship
Hoping another will patch it up with future progressions
One thing for sure is that perfectness is only a word
with a simple definition
With being in its true form of simple
Perfectness should look up to you
for a more powerful understanding of itself
So the only thing in sight that is needed is YOU

Take-In by the Hand

Man I don't know why the cars are moving so fast
These feet want to move forward
to get a glimpse of its other half
But there feels a hesitation
on whether or not it should move
The past found a way
to stamp insecurity on a wonder spirit
while looking for itself
The side to side confusion
has made logic contradict its own footsteps
So feelings and emotions can hold the courage
if the mind is willing to take shotgun for once
They say "he is supposed to be strong"
without realizing that the moon doesn't know itself
unless the Sun electrifies its opposite
It is the other side that is bringing uncertainty
It is the illusion of not shielding the heart
that makes vulnerability look promising
Yes, controlling the future
can be looked at as overbearing
Yes, reminiscing on the past
may force the indulging act of selfishness
But connection helped the mirror
to know that it really isn't that important
Or could it be
that it became the paintbrush to a blank canvas
Man, there is a problem
with not knowing what comes next

70

Take-In by the Hand *(Cont'd)*

He has a problem with demonstrating what he was taught
Since the shoes that are already filled aren't his own
With its original having a hard time
displaying the love that you need
Because society's VR goggles has become the Sunscreen
that you didn't need to put on to reflect the Sun
Since you show what true Sunrays are
before the sun starts to raise
How about you hold my hand for once?
Let go of the hate of self
because reflection is shown when light hits it and refract
Help me stay strong
so problem solving doesn't only become a job
Let this pride appreciate the beginning of survival
so he can show her something other than surviving
Therefore, strength is being demonstrated
to show the opposite of a nurturing aspect of creation
So be the one that shows that fighting is worth living
Yes, the dynamic of your size cannot be filled
But the texture of the shoe can be fulfilled
by the determination of his intention
Hopefully that anxiety to control
hasn't given up on the power that is still dormant
All that is needed
is for you to acknowledge that the sleeping giant
needs a reason to wake up

It's Getting Pretty Late

So, getting you along finally is accomplished
No need to seek any further for unwanted attention
How about we go for a walk outside?
Please say yes
so these butterflies in my stomach feel happiness
at the thought of holding your heart within my intentions
While applying no judgement towards past intuitions
Let me hold your hand
so jealousy can so jealousy can get mad at interaction
With your personal perfume not getting any attention
Smile can't help but to express its enjoyment
through bruised cheek bones that the cold contributed
Could it be
because your laugh makes losing thought as thoughtful?
Since reaction isn't as important as being
Therefore, I must pay close attention
to the intervals of your breathing
Would it be that I'm attracted
to the scent of you remembering yourself?
Since I'm interested in tasting something I can't see
Damn these feet of mine
keep losing their foot-in with reality
But my finger prints
get so eager with walking besides identical foot prints
Let me run my fingers through your hair
while you charge the pores on my skin
So being grounded isn't looked at as negative
Since I'm trying to hear every personal thought
that would make you blush

72

It's Getting Pretty Late *(Cont'd)*

My ears glued to the echo of you saying my name
in your own tone of voice
While feeling every syllable caressing my spirit
Like rubbing your hands together next to a flame
to keep warm
No need to explain
because imagination takes over sight since
Destiny has a cheat code that only involves duality
While these eyes of mine
finally got a glimpse of that anxiety disorder of
When you whisper in my ear "I only want you"
Does to this nervous system in conjunction with
the flow of "I think she is the One"
Man what a beautiful night it is
to watch the moon shine as you do
All the lamps above are crowding down to our energy
with the very same electricity that keeps them lit
Let me hold your shoes
so the cement beneath can get a proper definition of life
And I can sit back to watch as a seed plants itself
Here, take my jacket if you're cold
Or watch me lay it down over a puddle
So water can ripple out the need
for land to appreciate its mother attributes
While space above tries to partake in the identical race
that isn't part of our connection
So let the stars above becoming an organic GPS
to show us how to live outside of time

It's Getting Pretty Late *(Cont'd)*

Walking through this quicksand called life
in finding something real
And you dragging your feet through the mud of insecurities
in hope for something other than duty
So don't worry about the unknown because I'll save you
And I'm not worried about being different
Because you carry my flaws
with your genuine tears of enjoyment
So don't give in to the misfortunate of my name
And I won't care about what others think of you
Since our journey is to get back to each other
So let's not worry where we end up
Because the personal timeframe has our contract
with the signature of a similar sign language
based upon her curve with his arch
While the world around gets to take notes
with a pen and pad as its coach
So the scale's only function is the feather vs the heart
But, man it's getting dark, but why should this end already?
Walking down the block
with the future looking rather unattractive
Let's make today more special then yesterday
With the mind getting a backrow seat
because it thinks too much
While hopefully expressing the hunger
that this is only the beginning for us

Thru Shai's Eyes

To You

You are my light,
that shine so bright
You are the one that makes me turn blue
every time I see you
My heart is on a string so please don't let go!

When I am with you
I can cry
because you are life,
but I can leave out try
because it's not needed

Every time
that I'm not with you,
you know that
I'm with you
So you will always have a shoulder to lean on

you see that
I like you dearly
in this world
there isn't anything to fear see
you know that I am always thinking of what to brighten up
your day

To You *(Cont'd)*

when I'm with you it's my real self, no stage act,
no recorded lines, no being someone with you
and someone else when I'm with my friends
I know that by my actions that every time I'm with you

I speak the truth
you see that my eyes
drowned in happiness
when you come by
I like you very much and that isn't a lie

you brighten up my day
what more can I say

I Want to Understand

Ooh my goodness
A little girl is on the way
A beautiful sponge is coming
to soak up enough nutrients for life
A better version of the TV with no intention of control
Only giving his reality a shield against everyday chaos
Even if it is his own
Gentleness will be needed
to smooth out the rough edges from erosion
Forgiveness will be put on a loop
since we all were babies once
Pride will need to take a vacation
so portraying that "I'm wrong" will help bloom growth
since right or wrong is not greater than their bond
Patience will need to be injected into the veins
So sound can let sight have memories as well
So touch doesn't get overrated
because of hearing's connectedness
Communication has to be shown
with all its imperfections on call
In return development will progress simultaneously
Now the conversation will need to take place
without any rehearsed lines
Maybe something along these brain signals of
Wow, what a beautiful creation we've made
You will be protected from things
that are outside of the tunnel vision called young world

I Want to Understand *(Cont'd)*

Our history, yes, will moisturize your mind
like glazing a turkey for thanksgivings
You will be protected from what is not seen,
from wondering eyes
since they say
It Is Hard to Show an Old Dog New Tricks!
But memories will fuel these feet and make the experiences
worth more than capturing a picture
Click; your sincerity will be engraved into the mind
Click; I hope I'm not taking too many pics of your guidance
With showing the importance of failing and hard work
makes success a heartbeat away
The tough skin of your father
will rub off from continuous hugs and harsh reality views
While having a blind eye
to certain falls, tricking and making, tears less visible
But he will pick her up,
so pain won't find a host in this princess
Sometimes, he will humiliate his pride
in order for their closeness to become stronger
His arrogance will never have a say
since he too, is still learning
He may love from a distance
like a helicopter ride over viewing the city
So even when they are apart
the skin can still sense his warming presence
His over-standing the purpose of the world will not hinder
the outlook she will have on life

I Want to Understand *(Cont'd)*

Only sticky notes for when reality starts breaking down
Powerful words of encouragement will light her spirit high
Words like: "I am"
along with anything that the mind is capable of doing
So she can feel that he is near
and not there at the same time
Which would make any physical form jealous
So the bond between a father and his daughter
is more powerful than contemplated
Therefore, if confusion still arrives
then experience it through uninterrupted observation

Tryna Save My Liver

I need a sip first
Just enough
to whatever music that is playing makes my legs move
They say that the ones who say the truth the most are,
Drunken people, children, and old people
Be easy, will you
Let me take another sip
Just enough
for the brain to have a safe place
to break down this wall Called What if
That wraps itself around what it cannot control
of not knowing what happens next
Hold up, I need this next sip here
Just enough
so the toxicity makes my liver leaves,
therefore improves the truth
From the language they seem to call words
Okay, okay, I'm almost ready,
but let me take this last sip
Just enough
so as I'm talking I can feel your pupils dilating
Looking at this empty glass in my hand,
wondering if I should fill it up again
If I do,
then she will have to open my mind and listen to my soul
If I do,
she will have to digest my legacy

Tryna Save My Liver *(Cont'd)*

I'm not sure if she can imagine multiple times,
her experience flashing before her eyes
Or the tasty feeling of not touching herself
Wait, let's talk off camera for once
Exposing your secret uncontrollable sweaty imperfections
I need to get something off my chest first
I remembered the time
I beat the tidal wave in you
Or I remember
the space when I needed to be cleansed
So I, uh,
decided to jump straight forward into what I think is you
Or maybe I remember the time
everyone watched breakfast is served
No, not that one,
but the one right here between the car trains
But what if I fall baby
You'll have me forever,
so let time get a front row seat for once
Sit on the wind, while I make ink spills on your paper
I'm going to make you feel every letter of the alphabet
forward and backward
Remember when I gave you a message
and made you feel like water
I was obsessed with drinking all of you
So!
I know what it feels like to have you in my head

Tryna Save My Liver *(Cont'd)*

So!
I can taste the hairs on the upper part of the legs
Or could it be the
Wait...
pardon the vulgar frequency
Okay,
now where was I?
Or could it be
that I intentionally have a fantasy
with taking a bite into your
Universal Consciousness
So is that too much for you to absorb?
-
-
-
I hope not

Hand Print

Hey ma
Hey dad
I know I can be a lot at times
There are other times when I know,
but I still appreciate the discipline
I can be silly at some point in time
Just to keep your stress levels down
While praying to the unknown
to figure out what this body can do
I know that I lie every now and then
I'm still trying to figure out what is truth
and what should be left in the wind
But wait
I have a gift for you
No it isn't any drawing
No I'm not good at that even if you think different
And no it isn't a picture of me
I think you have enough of that already
I think the walls are comfortable with my face by now
I still don't like that picture you took of me
with the sweater that grandma gave me
I mean I like that she bought it
But she always buys me something I cannot fit
Yes, you taught me to be thankful for what I get
But when does my character over shine tradition
So, close your eyes and let wonder happen
Because this is what I made for you

Hand Print *(Cont'd)*

Which is my hand print in clay
It might not be much, but I know you need it
I hope it helps you relieve daily stress
I hope it shows you that you are loved
I don't have money yet,
but this imprint will live forever
My teacher told me that,
so I hope it becomes true
I know you have bills,
and I know you have to take care of me,
which can be pricey
Since my grandpa said
"children cost money"
So this hand print of mine
will be payment to all that you already have done
Think of it as a wonderful vacation away from work
Just use your imagination
Think of it like putting the car on cruise control
So the destination isn't as important as the journey
What is cruise control anyway?
Because I heard someone talking about
how his car has cruise control
Hopefully, it will keep them awake on the road,
so they don't fall asleep
You know how grandma falls asleep
in the middle of a movie

Hand Print *(Cont'd)*

I think she shouldn't work hard though,
because the job needs her
more than she needs that boring job
So can she play with me more
because I like the voices that she makes
Is it magic pa how she is able to change her voice?
Cause I'm having problems
with that big word called pronunciation
But this hand print that I made
will be with you always
Even if I get older
you will have youth to look back on
I don't know what that means
but it sounds really cool
I don't want to lose my thought
so I will end this with
I love you and come play with me already

Is Someone There?

Why do I feel like someone is on my shoulder?
Footprints behind me that aren't mine
Is that a clue or a misleading sign?
There is no way for someone to get in
Maybe the cracks inside the lies of how she got in
Maybe my imaginary glass breaking
that also was my defense system
Maybe the dog bark
that drown out the silent needles of deception
How come my shadow isn't behind or in front of me
Scars on the skin from verbal abuse
That somehow coexisted like tribal marks
Fire marks in the eyes from the false respect of another
Life messed up from the start
and the only way to purify it is to awake death
Body starting to disappear
from the crumbling of a picture of a case
that has been thrown out
Soul being copycatted from just a handshake
Spirit getting trapped in a conversation
about what to wear tomorrow
Standing next to you a crying
soul reads your mind
but yet he looks like you
but isn't you
just a mere illusion of what you're going to be

Is Someone There? *(Cont'd)*

Let lies tell you about a stranger
wanting to know about you
Because that person wants to be nice
Where is that sound coming from?
Maybe your mind
warning that someone is coming
Maybe your intellect
trying to break away
because it knows what is going to happen
Or maybe it's your conscience
actually playing a trick on you
Hug that person
and your pulse will become erased
Kiss that person
and watch your identity slip away
Tell that person you love him/her
and you won't have a life anymore
Just footsteps on the ground
to make noise that was transferred into a mp3 player
that had converted talk input into Listening format
So everyone can find out how that person left his world

Forceful Character

There is a problem with communication
that needs to put on display
It isn't the face to face dialect that needs technology
to monitor the interpretation that makes people think
that togetherness is important
It isn't the "in your face emotions" that lose connection
once feelings lose its way from over analyzing honesty
Or not even if loyalty stares you in the face
So that the authentic future isn't masked
by past unrehearsed dreams from clouded promises
Since words itself gets eaten up like false history
And the real truth is a pill that actually tastes bad
So one would wonder
what is the matter with this wandering soul?
Could it be
the false movie trailer that don't show true character?
Would it be
the arch of information that needs to go over one's head?
Or should it be
the pure intentions of one not wanting bad stereotypes
to inflict its poison like a regretful tattoo
who is still learning who that person really is
I guess it is the abilities of the person that gets overlooked
by others' withdrawal period
I guess it is the half-truth that becomes
the only information that deteriorate both sides

Forceful Character *(Cont'd)*

See people have a thing
with not going to the source to digest truth
It is more pleasurable
to grab a leaf from the wind and listen in
It's more comfortable
to swallow misguided but sweet scented lies
than accept the spirit that don't need the ego to co-sign
And it is the spoon feed connection
that gets misdirected with self-interest
Like stepping on everyone's toes
so self gets praised through an uninterested lens
While the other
forcefully consumes the backlash of someone else
who can't take responsibility for their own consequences
Maybe, just maybe
one day you will take ownership
for the unthoughtful sequences
That looked promising but in actuality
was only a creative illusion from someone's "one up"
on the individual's caring characteristic

TypO

So ah I have a problem with words
Not how to say them
Not the letters that form words
But the meaning of words
The behind the scenes words that have you feeling happy
While your subconscious feels the etymology of
it speaks another language
I have a problem with words
stringing your character on a billboard for everyone to see
For everyone to downplay and criticize
without both sides getting a turn to speak
Since there are three aspects:
your truth, their truth and the truth
I have a problem with words
grouping one past and presenting it inside a bender
With labeling it as being a total savage
Yes, it is true that we have: arm, leg, leg, arm, head
Yes, we can both think of what should be considered
right or wrong to a given situation
And yes we write our signature
with the same black ink for security
But we are way different from each other
Whether it is that we create and the other destroys
Or an original seems natural in itself
while the copycat appreciates duplication
Or how one is forced to survive to live
and the other survives outside of the meaning of survival
Man words go over my head like an upside down rainbow

TypO *(Cont'd)*

Don't know if it is a false painting
that became sunglasses to a screen watcher
Or a prediction
that was made by alternating the unseen generations
From egotistical hands that is eager to drop intelligence
While putting an imaginary gun to everyone else's head
to nurture it's off springs
See it is words that confuses people into thinking
they are weak on the 10 toes that they stand on
Into thinking that their minds cannot compete
with the purpose of money
Since money itself
is only but colored paper off of the bark of a tree
And the individual brings life to money
like breathing life into a flower to grow within darkness
But people have been pushed
into accepting only part of who they actually are
It's these words man
that have people giving power to something
that don't look like them
It's these words man
that can make or crush a person
Just by how you put each letter together
Since each letter can be interchangeable with another
And adding a belief system behind it as validation
In order to spread prosperity
or send them straight into despair

As You Were

Maybe researching the origin of words
isn't that bad as they be-lie-ve
As my body lay in this bed with the hand out
Looking for its reflection of what is considered comfort
With the other side pressed in
from what was used to be called the other half
And now wondering where that Knight in shining armor is
That shining armor
that is supposed to protect me from my own madness
Only these misfortunate covers
that seem to protect the cold
Not the cold weather but cold stares
that eyes can perceive that send a cold chill up the spine
So the cause is simple while frustrating gestures tend to be
puzzles to the eardrums
No communication arises to the surface
So please don't get mad at the heart
for not seeing your side of the argument
It is just that these tears have more compelling feelings
than your touch
Tears that is used as a defense mechanism for hurt
Hurt, from the protection plan
was bought to prevent broken love
That was paid for through commitment
Why, you ask?
Generations seems to repeat it self
While screaming "I'll never be like that person"

As You Were *(Cont'd)*

Only making your flaws more visible
like battle scars from childhood nightmares
Only making your footsteps seems more identical from
past reruns that should never been written
What happens next are judgmental beings
pointing a hatred finger at the accused
In return is labeled wrong
That wrong who was never given a job to a pure mind
So the blame becomes one sided like
believing the ozone layer is missed up from only factories
While behind closed doors
burning tonsils screaming for help
and that doesn't mean surgery
Mental and physical abuse that reached the skin
from buried answers and drowning trust
What was buried?
Dignity to tell what was never questioned
Dignity to never lead your partner astray
While spitefulness creeps up through the vents beneath
Beneath it all where lies have problems
sweeping the truth underneath the covers
Why is the trust drowning?
From unhappiness floating to the surface
From glassy words that don't seem strong
but have more value than self
With "I" being pumped through the veins
from this frozen heart

As You Were *(Cont'd)*

So blaming self has to be the other part
Accepting any situation
while pushing the consequences aside
like an annoying reporter
Letting fairy tale dreams cloud the mind
Letting thinking and acting on it
sink below the sole of the body
While words were meant to be
taken into consideration first
But having reason take a vacation
and letting emotions rob your insight
Insight, a strong ability that is over looked
In return the thought of a so called "good future"
becomes shades over the eyes
So once self is understood as simple
where is the fascination at?
Don't badmouth the want because it was fed and eaten up
like free food at a buffet line
Just note that replacement is always around the corner
Around the corner,
where that want can be opened up to any desires
Due to self having a change of heart
Not for the person but for the admired activity
And once reality sinks in like a poisonous snake bite
Self can only sit back in amazement
But remember
there was no gun pointed at overflowing flattery

As You Were *(Cont'd)*

But remember
that choices were made from persistence
and not caring about the outcome
Controlling the aura and shoots out confidence
to whoever wants or need it
So knowing what is wanted or needed
to be brought upfront
Or issues will be uncontrollably missed
like termites in the attic

You Gonna Let It Ring Forever

Ima just let it ring
So the person knows
what silence has a hard time emulating
Man, it is ringing that much?
But these feeling were already spilled out
like talking with a mouth full of Novocain
Man just let it go to voicemail already
Since it has more courage than these emotions
figuring out how it isn't important to a relationship
Maybe the person will notice that I'm not there
Even though these fingers only text
because voicemail don't seem normal
Since the promise of excepting your beauty
doesn't hold more acceptance than the like button
under your digital picture
Well if it keeps ringing,
then picking up can actually be looked at
as being emotional
Okay so if it keeps ringing,
then maybe the caller is looked at
as desperate
While not picking up
shows the side that the mask can't help but to visualize
Because it is afraid to show its true self
In order for the harsh reality of compliance
to be looked at as truthful

You Gonna Let It Ring Forever *(Cont'd)*

Since these feet made enough footprints in the sand
to give the return to sender enough evidence
that you are needed
But how about if the vibration of the phone
outweighs the importance of the call?
So the responsibility factor gets drowned out with
"I wonder why he didn't pick up for"
And maybe "I should call again"
to show the level of urgency
With these hands hesitating to swipe up
on the green button that exposed the sound to your voice
And sending the heart into a world wind of feelings
that the mind decided to hide based on protection
for the impulse that maybe the filter
whose job is to help beauty recognize itself
Is not needed in order for the reflection to actually exist
Since going deaf doesn't give an easy pass
from not hearing the cries
Since the cotton pushed into the ears only show negligence
And silence no longer needs ignorance
to demonstrate sound
So is!!
My ex ready to see that these footprints were made
so they don't always have to be in charge?
Is my ex ready to put the pride aside
to know that in order for greatest to see itself

You Gonna Let It Ring Forever *(Cont'd)*

The individual must go through trials and tribulations
to remember what was lost?
And could it be that the past shapes the present if you let it
Like realizing that if you keep wearing small shoes
you are bound to get bunions
While wondering
if my ex finally realized that the moon doesn't shine
until the sun demonstrates the opposite
Because words carry strength no matter who uses it
Therefore, what if the phone doesn't get picked up?
Hopefully, she has the determination to call again
and decides to drop this ideology of independence
Since its religion is separation
And let unity tell her that this definition of a man
cannot be put into words but only experienced
So duality can split into trinity
with the ability to become whole
While law and order has a set of values for creation to flow
So perfection only needs itself
to have it infinitely surrounding themselves
Now do you see why Completion is important?

You vs The Mask

I wish I could tell you how it's going to end
Or when it began
Well, got to start somewhere and let time unfold as it will
Now unlatch the strings of those boulders from individuals
with regret
Take off those shoes with more mileage
than any built automobile
Put the mirror in front so self can see
Don't get embarrassed
Remember now, you cannot listen with someone else's ears
So…
What is needed is an empty book
with enough pages to lose count
A chair without pride
A table that has a sense of imagination
and fiction as its guide
Something to write with that was taught by experience
And four walls that aren't there if you know they aren't
And last but not least, windows that never close
Because life is always breathing
Now let's speak self to yourself
without judgement for once
Let's let pride stay human
While looking at hate as being materialistic
It's a lot to digest at the moment I know but breathe
Now that we got that out of the way
Let's Talk

Unforeseen Church

Has anyone seen a real church before?
One that cares more than everyone else
Did anyone feel the energy of a real church?
That one where as soon as you step in
Electricity of simplicity tickling your feet
And whispering in your ears,
"You can call this home as well"
Can anyone express the truth
within the walls of the church?
The same truth
that your ancestors demonstrated through dance
Will anyone scream out their wrongdoings
without judging the less fortunate?
Well, hopefully everyone can realize
that they are part of each other
Since this DNA called the tree of life has many branches
With leaves full of integrity, will and courage
How come these papers filled of green hue
soak up the purpose?
Reasons rewritten with selfish morals
will only regenerate blinded zombies
Why are we so eager to call on a man-made phone?
If the true calling is repairing the broken hearted
Or the people with so many destinations,
but not the one back to their selves
What is with individuals
not standing for something that doesn't feel right?

Unforeseen Church *(Cont'd)*

It shows that someone is actually living for more than self
When will tithes and A.T.M. machines become extinct?
Becoming a family of one
with the sole purpose to protect and create
To spread happiness,
but doesn't hide the surroundings of corruption
Since there will always be evil vs. morality
Yes!! There are questions surfacing the mind
with answers right around the corner
Yes!!
The very thought of the church is under investigation
Yes!!
Those words are on the tip of the tongue
waiting to deflect this sunlight
Well the roots do need nutrients from the soil
to nurture a beautiful tree
If one of these questions
does not make one question their willful compass
That was manufactured by their church
Then there is a problem in its creation
Then the duty of togetherness has a malfunction
A reconfiguration is needed
in order to save the younger generations
And the ones that haven't been seen yet
A leader needs to be built with will, animosity for nature
Loss of materialistic success with the overstanding of it,
holds humanity back

Unforeseen Church *(Cont'd)*

And seeing into shades of complexions of the skin
as paint to different paint brushes,
to one canvas, called life's experience
A delegation with a mind of its own
With hands waiting for individuals to fall
While knowing that any quicksand
filled with depression and pain will not manifest
And spiteful human emotions
that causes them to think outside of unity
But sharing water from mother nature
that heals the mind as well as the soul
If this black print could be formed by unharmful ink
Then the garden full of seeds will begin to grow

Graffiti This Life

Watch with an open imagination of my world
Anyone can find it on walls of trucks
or on trains transporting life
that is capturing these footsteps
I cannot tell how the thoughts came
one in front of the another, like baby steps
But what could be revealed is the colors
that know more than emotions
Red, for the continuation of putting the body on the line,
so art can live
Orange, for the reputation that goes along with the name
Yellow, for the unlimited use of stencils for art to speak
Green, for the hearts that were caught in the mural itself
Blue, for the voice of speaking with silence
Purple, for the feelings of togetherness with each glance
White, for that 3-D effect that jumps at you
with the intention for a hug
Black, for the smiles
that has more value than any award imaginable
So the story of the journey is left
And the outside can imagine him or herself in the painting
It sprouts out the likely hood of
wanting to read The Suffering
It uncovers the identity of two different people
with the same sense of unity
Dance to the tunes of hip-hop
as it presents your life to you

Graffiti This Life *(Cont'd)*

While I graffiti my work on your heart
Rap to the lyrics that speaks every day commotions
While I make your jaw defy the laws of gravity
No need to try to talk over
or stamping a contradiction on the art
Or even trying to eliminate it
A snapshot or a standing ovation is enough respect, I say
Remember, this is not done for a paycheck
Rather justification of who I am so the world can see
From what others are willing to be
Therefore, a signature is formed
To know that faceless artist is me!
But again maybe it is you!

It Takes Two Hands to Clap

Some say that this journey is mine only to go on
Why yes, that is true
But you don't learn only by yourself
There are people who come on that same path
to learn and teach together
Some would believe that you are the reason
why you are successful within the career
That best describes you
Yeah, that is a good way to look at it
But make sure you give thanks
to the people who pushed you
To be the best version of yourself
No matter how many obstacles
that come in front of the dream
Some would think
that your pain cannot be duplicated
Or that no one understands the suffering
And you know what,
you are right about that one
But try to see it from a larger perspective
Even if the situation started differently
The outcome is the same
Either for it to happen again
or not happen again
And some would feel
that change only starts from within an individual

It Takes Two Hands to Clap *(Cont'd)*

Why yes, that is so true to say
See, the thing about change is that if a group of individuals
want the same process of change
and wants to do something about it
Then that is called democracy
It is the ability to put someone in power
to speak up for that group
To have somebody speak up for the voiceless
To make living in a land with honesty and dignity
being the driver of the car called unity
We are all part of a greater good of the people
We can all help one another to build up the confidence
And make a goal to eliminate insecurity
We all can think of ways
to make living more fulfilling and sustainable
so the next generations have a print set in stone
of multiple ways to improve society as a whole
While excluding one's own self-interest
Since it is about the well-being of everyone's lives
in the first place

Society's Glasses

These glasses have a really strong prescription
Group comfort,
to where if you are not down you are wrong
Group comfort,
to where thinking is looked at as obsolete
To where drama of others
is looked at as being exciting
To where going against the general population
is considered blasphemy
Guess these lenses was perfected to the T
With trial-n-error making the glass harder to break
And making the strap around the head seem soft
like your grandma's hand
While surveying human habit
with technology that has the most powerful fragrance
to keep individuals from using their minds
With their slogan being "We Will Do It for Them!"
Since thinking can be hard for certain people
Laziness is wrapped around most people
like a blanket in the winter looking for comfort
While the person doesn't realize that he or she is doing it
But then it isn't wrong to go left
when everyone is going right
It is ability to think like a leader than a statistic
Sometimes thinking like an individual is more valuable
It makes searching for the truth more desirable
like being 3 years old and eating your first candy

Society's Glasses *(Cont'd)*

There is a serious problem with these glasses
if reason hasn't surface yet
Maybe the glasses are too cool to take off
Maybe some people are afraid
to go against the masses
for a greater cause
Maybe, just maybe the work to take off the glasses
is overwhelming
The reason why the glasses are cool
is because everyone is wearing them
But you won't jump off the bridge
if everyone else does is right?
And then again it is better to stand out
like a sore thumb with an idea
than a needle in hay stack,
since a magnifying glass won't help
If you now see a complication,
then start with self
Overstand that seeing their soul through their eyes
has better judgment
than looking into dark shades.
It's like looking at shadows on the ground
Images will tend to change based on your perception
So detoxify your body from the poison
that was tasty to the consciousness
So detoxify your body from the poison
that made your mind think it was in control

Society's Glasses *(Cont'd)*

Not around self with leaders
that understood the false propaganda
And watch the road of redemption look fruitful
But be aware of ignorance
because it is lurking around the corner like scam artists

Stoneful Waves

Staring at those worldly curves
As they
paint a picture that the imagination can only endure
While its reflection makes any mirage jealous to thought
Gazing at those fruitful sounds hugging these eardrums
with the tonicity not understanding the meaning of words
While the frequency of the syllables
holds a strong bond between me and you
So wanting to touch
that see through thoughts of togetherness helps
Trying to sniff out that life of your scent
seems non-identical
How can one partake in painting the puzzle
that the imagination can hardly see?
Maybe making brushes seem like the desires
that the painters keep close
So the canvas can have its own future called children
So this ruff igneous rock
can actually be wrapped around this beautiful wave
With thinking like one and not two halves
Or maybe seeing oneself as creativity
or as destructive as the wind is to showing beauty
Or could be the waves
that formed a masterpiece of tasteful vibrations
with failing at trying to sketch its opposite

Stoneful Waves *(Cont'd)*

Since authenticity knows nothing of identical identity
until you introduce right to wrong
Therefore, don't force the rock to think
that a pebble is more important than where it came
And don't see the direction of the wave
as the final destination
for the stream to become a lake

Remorseful Thinking

I wonder if you can see
the conflicts that surrounds you
The same ones
that are being captured by cell phones
The same ones
on the TV screen
while abusing the repeat button
And the same ones
that are on the body cams of protection

I wonder if you noticed
the war that is being played under propaganda
The players aren't hidden
Well, some are,
to confuse the definition between predator and prey
The system isn't hidden
Its co-existing in plain sight
But nothing is being done about the two

I wonder if the killing
is making an impact on the subconscious
the way it floods YouTube or Facebook
Did that sink yet?
But, it does have a purpose
and it is to store fear inside
To make you think you know
To show survival without morality

Remorseful Thinking *(Cont'd)*

I wonder if anyone has noticed
that animals survive and humans supposed to live
Since animals move on instinct only
While human beings
have the choice to think and then react
based on one's understanding of who they are,
or someone who chose to become
There is much power in sending
either positive or negative energy out into the universe

You get what you give out
Yet individuals praise their job more than themselves
One's life is more important
than something that is man-made
But then it makes one wonder
is living a thing of the past ?
And that, my friend,
is a dangerous situation to be in

The fact that one may or may not know
who they naturally are is a serious problem
They're thoughtfully hateful obstacles
placed in front of the eyes even if you don't care to see
Or has chosen comfortability as a scapegoat
The only person you are running away from Is YOU
That same self that is being
bombarded with self-hate algorithms

Remorseful Thinking *(Cont'd)*

Like what Neo was facing
in the movie The Matrix
There is a path that everyone is on which can help
And that is to be yourself for a change
Appreciate the power
of having to think an action and watch it unfold
Grasp the extraordinary joy
of knowing and of forgiving one's intentions
rather than what they went through

Feel the blessings
of the ability of not knowing what "supremacy" was
Before leaving the mother's womb
Therefore,
Be what you are born to be
Like nature understands
what the earth and water together means
So all I know is
Be You!

Ungrateful Games

Things are not the same anymore
Roles are playing hop scotch with genders
So her and him are forced to change their shoe size
While things used to be simple
Yet simple is looked at as being "Overrated"
With fun being the only instrument
that is helping this fire burn
Now and only now
is the gasoline for a healthy forest to burn
While flowers, talk, and closure gets neglected
Flowers' fragrances
are getting pushed aside for green backs
Talk or better yet conversation
somehow falls into the same category as
"all in your feelings"
Closure will never get remorse
because that "live for the moment" stage is in effect
will always outshine spending time
Spending time, which can be a remedy for a frozen heart
that is blindly reminded that every man is the same
With women being on a mission
to think like men
While men
are acting like women without a warning caution
People are cooking with the wrong ingredients
So don't be surprised if you get sick
Since the balance has accepted being lopsided

Ungrateful Games *(Cont'd)*

Soo!!!
Is there a problem in the near future?
Yes!
It becomes normal to the masses
Some will cling onto the idea of
"fun" like a moth to a flame
Some will adopt the idea
that they will be young forever
Others will be
pushed into motion only from their emotions
and will do more harm than good
With full of thoughts
from grudges harboring the brain
like new hair growth
Yes, shaving it all off would be beneficial
but once that thought is there
it will always grow back
Since you aren't supposed to kill the weed
But nurture the soil underneath the cement
So what is the purpose of mental change?
Being honest with your voice
so detox can know its true enemy
Understanding what the heart
needs rather than wants
Understanding that the mind
needs cleansing just as much as the organs do
Accepting what was done in the past being the pamphlet

Ungrateful Games *(Cont'd)*

So the next time
having an idea of what not to do for the sake of identity
So now it can see
that the wall is detrimental based on past experience
I mean sunshine can't seep through
if the blinds are fighting the light
It is time for the hard part that we don't want to do
With stop predicting the future
and work on the moment
until living for each other becomes natural
Don't be afraid to hit a bump in the road
Or maybe lose sight of self while discovering self
The road was never built smooth to begin with
But accept someone who is willing to patch up your road

Fogy Footprints

I left my breath in the footprints
with knowing that pain can take over
the sound waves of communication at any instance
So!! Let's see if the past is an aggressive manuscript
looking for its star recipient
Hearing the counterfeit monotone frequency
that issued the feet to move without common
Common sense, that hasn't overturned every stone
While touching a duplicate that is allergic to its original
So taste cannot comprehend the purpose of photosynthesis
Because human nature is a byproduct of repetition
Because this life syringe called life isn't enough information
to tell why the last generation is afraid of truth
Which cannot demonstrate
why your answers involve their past quicksand images
While smelling lies thru tough love made railroad tracks of
Making "CLEAR!" hard to understand while electricity
tries to connect individuality with the cold
The blueprint mad at its creation
Yes, the chain of continuity isn't broken
Yes, the born equilibrium
is forced to live in the reflection of ghost stories
Because the truth
is cuddled like a new born with more shots than its age
Because protection seems to hate you
way more than protecting you
So when will the footprints in front
not be looked at as a dis-ease

Happy Mother's Year (Pt. 1)

We understand the time
We understood the place
Both of these words cannot match to who you are

The watcher of the night
from the vibrations of her cubs near by

Even when you felt alone
there was a blanket of care shielding you

Even if crushed dreams appear too often
there will always be a soft voice saying
"Everything will be alright"

One hug
seems closer to perfect than your own skin
One kiss
feels healthier than any medicine imaginable

So stand up
for the sacrifices that only felt normal
Normal, from a stranger looking in the window
seeming hard

So stand up
for making the words "quiet down" the tools
for which we use our 2 ears more than our mouth

Happy Mother's Year (Pt. 1) *(Cont'd)*

From the beginning,
that fragrance kept us out of danger;
not only the voice alone

From when we were small,
band aids never had more value than your touch
they only looked cool to show off to the other kids

From discovering who we are as teens
Rebelling only made your love stronger than these
understandable cuffs called "peer pressure"
that bound us in having fun

Being looked at as
more important than standing alone in a sea of twins

From becoming an adult
some try to make a better version of her in them self

While others use her as a building block
for connecting with the past so the present

Won't have conflicts with what the future holds
Or should I say what her spirit through you holds

I Am

I am pain that is sold to unfaithful tears
I am the wind's vision
I am hidden underneath chaos and anger
I am an unknown spirit to my own existence
I am tears that leak out of the eyes but never falls
I am the only one that can't love
I am the real story that people just shove under the cover
I am the soul that shadow's people voices
I am the clown's tears
I am the shadow on the wall
I am fear that moves like it's unclear
I am voices that people don't pay attention to,
so when I talk
it's like a buzzing sound in their ear
I am silent choices that people over look
I am a person waiting to be discovered

1566 Eastern Parkway

I'm a
Kind of blushing these emotions into words
I'm a
Anxious to explain how this smile is still a smile
I'm a
Hoping to not lose anyone with those journey footprints
that tend to leave craters behind
Let's go back to the reasons for being me
No mirror required
Authenticity was engraved in the sole
So these feet always had a pair
Speaking words may sound loud
But I'm expressing what feels wrong
Fighting with anger
so this small body doesn't get overlooked
Therefore, the bodyguard from within
makes protection priceless
Speaking up and fighting for others
is my definition of care
Hanging around with the older cats who did things
So that word called "sucker"
never magically appears on my forehead
Hey... hey
Remember the times she snuck in the movie theatres
to watch pimps do martial arts
Or we would laugh at how the people are not getting hit
while sound effects still came out

1566 Eastern Parkway *(Cont'd)*

Or that movie "Black Belt Jones" and "Dolemite"
with the brother who could rhyme any word
and make it look good also
I know everyone remembers "Foxy Brown"
with Pam Grier in it
Either all the boys wanted to date her
or all the girls wanted to be her
See me, I didn't want to be her because I looked good
Brick House
But before Brue Lee, that was what we had
When it did come to our theatres,
which was "Fighter Bruce Lee"
Nay know, right sis
That movie made us feel like we were missing out
Now music is part of me like family through these veins
Give me a beat, then the song is yours
The style of clothes worn
Tight but the image means everything with being in
But this creation here, flawless to touch
I mean "Don't touch it aight"
And that Afro was Far out!
The message was still potent
Segregation is an ugly thing
and I stand up for my brothers and sisters
who fought against the injustice of police brutality
Seeing people die in front of my eyes is not pretty
But all helped mold the queen into loyalty
and loss of bull-shh

1566 Eastern Parkway *(Cont'd)*

Also, bringing a young king into this world
that brings faucet tears of joy
Shedding strengths to sow in with his
So a veil foresees the questions he must answer
While love and experience shares binoculars
to watch out for hypocrites

Regain A Life

Breathe easy now
No more crying…please
Tease your mind with happiness
My fault was not your tragedy
Your own got the best of you
Blue skies swept the feet beneath
and forced the tears to drip
As kindness slips under the radar
to change an outcome

Dear Son

Come
Come next to me and speak your mind
Let insecurity become a stranger at the door
Let acting like your funny classmate
become a wandering soul without a body
I'm going to let you know a couple of things about life
Once the words leave this strong voice
and catch it like the value of a Dreamcatcher
Let me change the tone of sound
so not only your hair on the skin receive it,
but your spirit as well so it can be a teacher to itself
We are here in this world
to look for who we want to be
Caged in the visible yet human land
that hasn't understood anything so far
Far away in sight wishing for guidance from the elders
And also wanted to teach the same elders harmony
You must not steer away from who you are
Even if the identity of everyone else
likes who they have become
You are strong beyond thought
Fear will seem to exit once you see yourself
You become an unmovable force
But as gentle as a flower
loving the destination of the wind
You will feel the strength of the trees,
bringing the soul life

Dear Son *(Cont'd)*

You will sense the water becoming the architect
for the rock's canvas
The power of chasing is not thinking about the chase itself
Rather the discovery of what is comfortable to the 5 senses
You are brave my son
Know that bullets only scar the body
because that is the only place it feels
You are brave to stand
when everyone else sits in despair
You are more brave than your father
Since he was forced to think
and you have a choice of what to think
Brave only overstands
when you do it unintentionally
Since it is only a feeling
It can only have value once self recognizes it
You must see thy self as only one with two halves
The journey of life is to find who you are
And not what you have endured
My son
Know that letting go does not mean you are giving up
You've got the vision to see what is worth a fight
And what is lost in itself
You are a King my son
You write books without lifting a pen
If anyone wants to read the footprints
they must let go of their pride

Dear Son *(Cont'd)*

Son, you must realize
that some people will put pride before love
Love which one can feel
more heartwarming than the purpose of a hug
Not everyone is your friend
Not everyone is your enemy
If they are willing to be spiteful to a gift
of whatever it is than a warm full palm
Then an invisible knife
will always be in their back pocket
Son
You must trust your soul when looking for answers
At least it will always tell the truth
Even if it is hard to hold on to
This world I brought you in is having a difficult time
believing that individuals have the same powers
as the superheroes in these comic books
My mission is to help you grow into yourself
and let you know
that it is okay to express your hidden feelings
To shed the emotions that stop your tears from flowing
I cannot tell you everything that one needs to know
But!!!!
I can tell you that I Love You
And I'll pick you up after every fall
And tough love itself will envy the true nature of care

Tried My Best

Let it Ring Forever

Ring!
Ring!
Ring!
Man just let it go to voicemail
Since this voice seems more important
when it becomes repetitive
So that person knows the feeling of vulnerability
Since the past and the present
has a hard time distinguishing the difference
with what has already hurt and what it will hurt
Not self, but the consciousness, which has a difficult time
coping between you and me,
since we both come from the same source
So let's put it on display,
so the insecurity of not being nurtured
and not remembering the imagine
of what the divine supposed to embody
while offering the way out from the norm
That most have a hard time deciphering its opposite from
The normal sense that needs the mind to not think,
but they wonder
why the call never gets picked up while considering
Could it be that the attention is glorified like a rainbow?
Since its intentions is to go over everyone's head
Since in order to trick most people
you have to make it look non-real
Or can it be that money has become more attractive?
Yet these words' only interest is in shaking the paradox
that has groomed your thinking

Temporarily Pills

Wash my face in this water of regret
Lift the head to see the image that I became in the mirror
Scars from your past cling to my skin like broken clamps
Hands like a 70-year-old man
because of everything that was taken away
Eyes that haven't felt what still feels like,
but only a jack hammer pressed up again concrete
Ears lost to that ringing sound,
like when you listen to loud music for a long time
Tongue lost connection to taste
like a cell phone tower built in a rain forest
As I picked up this bottle it has a small print that says
"CAUTION" may cause your future to disappear
Pop two pills into my mouth
with the past heading for the future
Here it goes
You took it all with my help
While hands from every direction
are pulling us apart for our own good
Carved "you and me" in this wood
that childhood memories walk daily for
Bore my skin to reach my heart
where the happiness that you was supposed to give me was
Plea my undying love into the wrong drain,
I guess the sound waves couldn't touch the hear drums
Only tums that made to stop bloating
Secrets that was kept close
were a merely jokes to tickle your taste buds

Temporarily Pills *(Cont'd)*

Tears that dropped from the clouds,
were caught by this flexible shoulder
Proved to be, in return acid rain particles
that decided to expose my weakness
Ears left the face
from the amount of information that was irrelevant
Irrelevant truth that the mouth is not used to use
Bruise lies that became its first language
Like writing you're "ABC's"
Acknowledge your crime
with the hand of help patting the back
Because life does not only move to the beat of the feet
Continue along this white brick road and watch;
Watch the crumbling of that so called special someone
drinking his or her self to the soil
To where people have a habit to look down on
As I sit in this empty tub
with my hands on my cheeks
I wonder
Slumber into deep sleep
With everything going down the pipes
besides the water
Imagining the tight grip that held you close
and as well as pushing you away
Then I opened my eyes
and wondered how could I do this to
A PRIZE LIKE YOU

Is This the End?

Man we been here for some time now
You are my soul mate
with the thought of you believing in me
With the ring
only symbolizing the bond that your mind needs
So she is put 1st in his heart over everyone else
Yet distance is becoming a program
that we didn't sign up for
Play fights turn into arguments of disappointment
Smiles becomes tears of a clown
And no one wants to unmask that clown
Conversations becoming lost scrolls in the sand
like buried treasure
While our kids hold the treasure maps in their lives
I wonder when the kids' future will become a top priority
So life can rekindle that candle flame that was blown out
by what you wonder?
Thinking like individuals rather than as we
Assuming the worse rather than talking it out like adults
As we walk
Footsteps in the ground
starting to look invisible to my eyes
While looking clear to intruders
Slick moves like showing the single status
always find itself floating to surface
Surface, because
the truth has a way with slipping through the cracks

Is This the End? *(Cont'd)*

So the light at the end of the tunnel goes to the kids
The kids that once held that thin bond
That is slowly breaking only in the wife's vision
due to the fact that she hates wearing glasses
We as a team seem to have a strong hand
in the cookie jar of infidelity
Think that is bad?
Bad from the others
looking through the cracks in the walls
of heated arguments
No hand to hand combat,
jus unhealthy words that effect the mental
The bed seems more strange due to the fact
that not even there can we come together as a couple
The only joy comes from
the crooked smiles that tend to be genuine
Or the moments that are not made around each other
Is this the end?
Of you and I
Of this marriage that was held for 15 years' now
Honey you can help me out if I'm wrong here
If I'm wrong here, then maybe it is the end
End of your smile that keeps me sane
End of you making feel like
I'm right when I am actually wrong
End of looking into our own future
held by the glare in your eyes

Is This the End? *(Cont'd)*

And the end of our children believing in just maybe
We can pull it out in the end
Time cannot tell how this moment became so strange
And the future as well,
since the present is only relevant
in the chapters called "Life"
Maybe we need someone outside our relationship
to tell us what is wrong
Maybe we need to listen to our kids more
Or maybe this feeling is only temporary
The only thing that is certain
is either we are made for each other
through all the commotion
Or being apart is healthier for the both of us
Just don't let the nightmares continue
when the dreams start to feel like reality

Fast Heartbeat Without

These sweaty hands
were supposed to bring you a letter of happiness
But instead my numb logic reasoning
gets flooded by my feelings
I want to express electric attraction I have for you
The same attraction that the hair has
when a balloon has static electricity
I want to express the adrenaline rush your voice does to me
Like jumping off a mountain for the first time
and not caring what happens next
No need to question
where this smile on my chest comes from
No need to understand
why compliments flow out of my mouth like the Nile River
If confusion still lingers
around wondering why the heart beats fast
Then listen a little bit longer
It starts with the personality being so personally interesting
like learning a new language
With the future wrapped all around it
like the soul is intertwined with its body
After that comes that elegant perfume
which has a lasso on the sense of smell
that pulls the feet in the direction
from what the heart can sense like motion sensors

Fast Heartbeat Without *(Cont'd)*

Don't smile from the mouth
but let the eyes smile more
This shows that the ears are listening to every detail
that the heart is spilling out on a canvas
I love you forever
love is never lost
If not reciprocated it will flow back
and soften and purify the heart

Not So Far Gone

At night with the open sky looking at me
Let's talk for a minute
A fallen solider has left this world
but the grace he left us has heart beats
He was a father that taught his children right from wrong
To believe in themselves and show the world their talent
Signs are controlling my feeling
to where other people can sense it too
I can't talk to the clouds above
Because the clouds are like time
passing me by even if I'm not moving
Something that didn't pass
was the food that heated up our stomachs
A chef that did not need a degree
to show a masterpiece through food
Memories that will continue to grasp their taste buds
like life traveling into new generations
My heart is looking for a miracle
That same miracle that a brother and sister shares
Verbal agreements and disagreements
like throwing up a quarter
and not caring where it lands.
Play fights in showing who is stronger
But in return
it shows the level of loves between the both of them
With touching

Not So Far Gone *(Cont'd)*

Touching people
on the other hand being fulfilling to the soul
It shows that you made a difference in someone's life
like giving a reason to live
It also shows that he wants to live for someone
other than himself
Wow!
How great is that
I'll tell you
Amazing

Too Much Daydreaming

Is this real
or just a trick that I have no control of
Is there like between us
or fish that got caught on the line
Smiles that say you can be someone for me
Or a game being played by one controller
Heart beats fast by the sound of a giggle
All senses lost except sight
because eyes don't want to miss anything

Is this a happy beginning
that future wants to look forward too?
Or an ending
that one only knows the outcome
They say trust your heart on things
and that will guide you
But what if
that so called heart
can only beat from feelings alone

Daydreaming is what keeps me sleep
while my brain thinks it's active
While the reality part is needed
because that is where life is moving
Self has to be pulled together
because the present is the opening to the future
where feelings and stupidity seem to go hand to hand

Too Much Daydreaming *(Cont'd)*

But the hard part is
that the walls around see that
once someone's life is put into other person's hands,
there is no letting go
unless you say
I'm squeezing too tight

Will you lead to the road to opportunity?
Or where everyone else has failed
Knowing that predictions from another
only blinds the eyes
like a baby in the womb
And looking to the sky for advice
only slows you up
while everyone is passing by

So the question
that is pretty readable on the forehead is
Is this real
or other reason
to make the heart colder than it already is?

The Letter Attached

At the window with no lead of where you are
No one around to listen to my story
The paper on the table becomes my only companion
Nothing else to do but face away from the world
I start to write
"The Letter" by my heart
Hello there;
Looking for a shine on my face,
I speak to you
Where have you gone?
When will my life return to give me some hope?
I'm trying to live with an agenda on my brain
Looking into other people's hearts
to find what you give to me
Every time I say hi to you
You are the only one who can raise my spirit
While others
try to help put what cannot be glued together
It's like a puzzle with three missing pieces;
love, happiness and comfort
When can your heart join mine?
Letting us become one
like how it's supposed to be
But yet
I'm not sure of how the future will turn out to be
Hearts get shattered, minds get lost
And then you're back at square one

The Letter Attached *(Cont'd)*

But then again I'm fine when I speak to you
My heart beat fast whenever there is a smile
Let me know if I'm close
because I wouldn't know
Please pick up the pencil and spill your heart to me
Because I don't feel normal
Wiping the tears away from my face
Because I know you would for me
Why are tears rolling down on my face?
Because my eye lids aren't as strong as this paper
that is holding my emotions together
Are we a match made in heaven?
Or a couple on earth?
Sitting on the steps
while the rain tries to be a wet blanket
Waiting
for the mail carrier to give me a sign of relief

The Key

Knock...Knock...Knock
Will you let me in?
In those four chambers of your own life
The one everybody wants to be a part of
or abuse from confusion
Because they are not strong enough
to hold up amazement
And showing off the prize
like a little kid unwrapping a present for Christmas
While dancing in front of the camera
External features are only the wrapping paper
to the gift inside
While your strong, will and mind
being the ribbons for everyone to see
Believe in what you have as your rock
Block those negative manipulators
As I brag to Mother Nature saying
"She is brighter than your sun-rays in the morning"
Taunting the wind by saying
"I swept her off her feet
faster than you can sweep a building
going one hundred miles per hour"
Talking down to the ground saying
"She is stronger than the substances that put you together"
Games of hoops put in front to test faith and destiny
If failed, judgment covered the eyes
like cement covering a broken pothole

144

The Key *(Cont'd)*

Captain America shield state of mind
with the impression of
"I Do Not Care"
scares off many
While others laugh with the impression of
"Stay by Yourself Then" tickle their vocal cords
Trust in what the future can bring to your doorstep
Choose not
and dwell on the past
for having a voice in everything that was wanted
Wanted from dreams
that drew a sketch of what life supposed to color in
To show the desired painting
The Key to your heart,
needed to complete the journey
No running after faded footsteps in the sand
Footsteps that disappear when you sense I am near
No waiting on every hand and foot
like I am qualified to become a butler
Yes, maybe on every hand and foot,
not a paid butler,
but only when we become equal
I want
what most people only see as a mirage
I want
what most people come close to,
like a word on the tip of their tongue

The Key *(Cont'd)*

You want
to feel something real
Real to where bragging comes natural
You want
what your grandmother's stories portray as the right person
Right person, not the one that wants a fairytale ending
The one that wants to take you away from the norm
So take the leap because there is no ground underneath
With only our guidance controlling the path we try
Do you feel comfortable now to let go?
To give The Key to your other half
The other half
that made that same promise in the beginning
With the word "L-O-V-E"
getting jealous of our own version of love
No clouded judgment needed
Only room for improvement being our hustle
So as I attempt to stop time for a quick minute
I ask you
with my heart beating on my sleeve
Are you ready to take this dive with me?

Robert Horry vs. John Starks(Win or Lose)

Some people don't understand how we play this life
Many different strategies to survive
Many different stepping stone to push you higher
All depends on what you are stepping on
While others will try to put their two cents in a machine
that only accepts quarters
They will make decisions on the outcome
Not the role
Not the contribution to the outcome
But what looks good to the naked eye
Since those eyes do like entertainment
So judgmental thoughts will start to bubble
Because that third eye was never trained to see
like the ones that open and closes
Listen with your hears and feel these words
Sometimes the most difficult task has only one name on it
That name is as strong as cement
Or as elastic as a bungee cord hugging onto life effortlessly
That person is called to make impossible look easy
That person is called to only finish what they started
The position was carved
from the execution in the small window being open
Peyton Manning is good at that
No need for a lot of time being needed is their specialty
With their backs being up against the wall showing comfort
Like a couch potato
concerned only about himself plus one equals the television
I guess tunnel vision
is a mechanism for on track development

147

Robert Horry vs. John Starks(Win or Lose)*Cont'd)*

But some will never grasp that superhuman trait
See now there is that other side
that people will see without any directions
They will cling onto it for dear life
All for that adrenaline high
to make them feel part of the team they watch
As the person needs no introduction to make the right play
The team will be put on the shoulder for safe keeping
if necessary
They will do everything that is humanly impossible
While window shoppers cannot see past their mentality
So they will be looked at as great
They will be looked at as a cash cow
They will always come up in discussions as
Why didn't that person win?
Or how come nobody else chipped in?
Well some will never know
what blood, sweat, and tears that was kept bottled up
No one will understand
the injuries the mind and body had to go through
Allen Iverson was another trade mark of that
Only but so much can be done
without the company of others
A song is not but a song by words alone
So some will lose but not by your standards
And others will win by the proper role they take

I'm Falling into Life

Open your eyes and to the pressure of the fact
That I can't stop falling
I am upside down with my heart in my mouth from shock
Tears roll upward towards my mind
Images upside down because I'm right side up
Clouds coming closer to me
Rain next to me, falling the same way as I am
But which way am I falling
I hold on to my spirit by my fingertips
as it keeps on telling me
I'm sorry I have to leave
It talks to me again
We weren't meant to be together
Eyes drying up from the lack of water
Sensitivity in my body goes numb
The sense of smile is screaming for the opposite
No more imaginary friend
to guide me from the truth
No more false feelings
to keep of the person you used to like
The wind
doesn't want to protect me from the ground anymore
Cloud 9
isn't available to hold my feelings in now
Mind trying to come back to earth
like my body because it's a drifter
But the drifting ability is no longer active

I'm Falling into Life *(Cont'd)*

Thinking to the clouds isn't a place to call home anymore
The endless pain of hitting the ground
is the only thing with open arms
Dreams no longer tell stories
because you've seen them all
Mind can't hold on to imaginary words
because they found the key to the lock
Can't watch TV
because you lived through every drama
Floor feels uncomfortable
because the ceiling was the first place where I stood
Skin starting to peel from the speed of falling
Will I hit the ground before my heart stops beating?
Or will my heart stop beating before I hit the ground?
Am I falling to the ground or to the sky?
If it's the ground, get ready to open your mouth
because your skin is too strong for my body
If it's the sky open your mind
because mine decided to leave
Feel the burn as I get close to the world
Scared and yet happy at the same time

Poetry

Rain drops on the flower…
Feels its form as the water regenerates life…
Roots grabs the soil close like veins hugs the heart…
Imagine the pulse it gives off
as the pores in skin move 2 the motion of perfection…
Hands move through the sense of sight
because touch is already given…
Feet drag across life's nature
because everything underneath is nonexistent…
Hair trapped in the scalp
because if it separates
then it won't know y its living…
Brain is like the stem of the flower…
Everything has to go through it
in order to flow calmly while everything around tries to
alter balance…
Yo I can keep going 2 if I want…
I feel you on that thou Carfax the conversation like this…
Table of life I sit down at…
The chair of chance I'll hope to meet…
Greet the folks of never
that is held in the right hand
and spoon of love
becomes the ingredients in the other hand
What is on this table that concerns my soul?…

Poetry *(Cont'd)*

Life controls the table…
But control disrupts the material that makes it…
Will I eat what I can't brain wash??…
Yes, I will consume it while you all call me crazy…
Maybe lazy moves my feet or fleet to death
so I won't hear a response…
Never mind the blah blah blah
because I already taught your attention

Heru Smith started spilling his unsettled feelings when he was thirteen years old, but it was his eight-grade poetry teacher who pushed him to use words to express what is on his mind. He doubted what she saw in him because he was still figuring out who he wanted to become. Once he was about 25 years of age he was going through struggles with how he was born and the feelings that come along with being so-called different. And these emotions felt difficult, so he decided to write his pain out on paper to calm down his spirit. Therefore, you are getting his perspective on what he painfully went through, and hopefully, it helps you find peace with whatever you are attempting to get over.

CONTACT

Email: MrSmith2K@gmail.com
IG: @Capital.ru
Facebook: Shai Nefer Heru

Look for:
Thru Shais's Eyes II

Made in the USA
Middletown, DE
09 September 2023

37860268R00093